WOMEN
MEAN
BUSINESS

WOMEN
MEAN
BUSINESS

One Woman's Journey
into Entrepreneurship

ROSEMARY DELANEY

ORPEN PRESS

Published by
ORPEN PRESS
Lonsdale House
Avoca Avenue
Blackrock
Co. Dublin
Ireland

e-mail: info@orpenpress.com
www.orpenpress.com

© Rosemary Delaney, 2011

ISBN: 978-1-871305-25-8

Printed in the UK by CPI Antony Rowe.

This book is dedicated to my husband David – thank you for completing my world; to Hannah and Lydia who are growing up too fast for words; and to Rebecca who believes she is a princess, an inventor and a budding publisher – and all at the ripe old age of six. May you always follow your dreams and believe.

Contents

	Preface	ix
	Introduction	1
Chapter 1	Just Do It!	9
Chapter 2	The Glass Illusion	16
Chapter 3	The Power of the Notebook	29
Chapter 4	From Boardroom to Bedroom	41
Chapter 5	Keep It Dynamic Stupid (KIDS)	55
Chapter 6	Failure Is Not an Option	71
Chapter 7	All Red but Where's the Black – Cash Flows and more Cash Flows	84
Chapter 8	Waistlines and Deadlines – The Yo-Yo Diet of a Stressed Businesswoman	100
Chapter 9	Role Models – They Come in Different Sizes!	114
Chapter 10	Loving Your Work	125
Chapter 11	Is the Price Right?	137
Chapter 12	Time for Change	151
	Further Reading	164

Preface

ARE YOU LIVING the dream? Do you wake up each morning with a smile on your face as you turn to kiss the one you love? Do you constantly have a spring in your stride and automatically walk tall? Or perhaps every morning is like Monday morning for you, when you wake with that pit-in-your-stomach feeling. You like to think it's a hunger pain, but it persists even after breakfast. As you get on the bus, drive your car or cycle your little legs off, it's still hanging around. And when you get to your place of work, the pain gets a bit stronger to the point when you can't control it. You feel physically sick, like the feeling you get before an exam. One part of you knows what it is but you won't admit it to yourself because you feel trapped. Yes, you hate your job, you hate your life and you see no way out. What if I told you that you're not alone and that this feeling is shared by thousands – hundreds of thousands – of people living and working around you? And what if I told you to stop, take a deep breath, and get up and walk away?

Welcome to my world. It may have taken me a decade or so to take the leap of faith – to set up my own business – but I haven't looked back. Yes, I missed the fat salary – initially. But in return I gained the freedom to sink or swim on my own merit. Five years ago I fulfilled one of my main ambitions in life when I launched my own magazine. *Women Mean Business* (*WMB*) (womenmean business.com) was the first title in the Irish marketplace targeted at businesswomen and female entrepreneurs. Had I thought too long or too hard about the 'how' and 'why', I probably would have failed before I started. In the intervening years I've built a successful brand which extends to conferencing, contract publishing and multimedia offerings. I've attracted a credible list of blue-chip clients and met inspiring men and women along the way.

I am building on the foundations of my business and, as I have learned many lessons along the way, I thought I'd share some of them in the hope that they would encourage, inspire and motivate others to believe and to take the leap. One of my other life goals was to write a book and, as fate would intervene, it is this book.

Women Mean Business: One Woman's Journey into Entrepreneursahip is for all those passionate women who dare to believe that they can make a difference in the world around them. It's a book of reflection, a book of lessons learned by a woman who wears her heart on her sleeve! *Women Mean Business* is all about the Business of Women – the challenges, solutions and trade-offs, the battles lost and won. It gives an honest insight into my journey into entrepreneurship and my continuous search for a more balanced and fulfilled life. There are barriers to break, mountains to climb, moments of doubt, and there are more disappointments than wins, sometimes.

If you are a stay-at-home mum who might want to return to work, a recent graduate who wants to forge a career for life, a businesswoman who is looking for balance without having to compromise to the extreme, a women considering the world of entrepreneurship or someone who just wants to be part of a growing network for positive change, this is the read for you.

This is my story. It is far from complete. It doesn't pretend to be a story of success or by someone of celebrity status. I'm just a person who refuses to give up on her dreams – and I have many. As one of my life goals is reached, another appears from the shadows as if waiting its turn in the queue. It is a personal story where I leave myself open to scrutiny. But not by strangers, hopefully by like-minded individuals who will accept me, warts and all; who can identify with the trials and tribulations of life and perhaps nod knowingly at times when my familiar is also their familiar. As my dream to establish a brand based around businesswomen and female entrepreneurs is unique, so too is this story. It is less a 'how to' book than a 'why not?' book. It is positive for the most part because I am positive for the most part. There are many useful messages in its lines for those willing to read between them.

Introduction

W E HAVE ALL EXPERIENCED that gut feeling, that intuitive 'niggling', when our little but larger-than-life 'inner voice' whispers: 'It's the right time. It's now. Just do it!' No, I'm not mad – you know you have one too. The only difference between you, me and millions of others is that some of us choose to block out our inner voice, whereas others embrace it.

My mind works 24/7, 365 days of the year – I think extra hard in a leap year. The word 'random', which is soooo popular with our facebooking, tweeting, socially savvy teenagers of today, is exactly how I would describe my inner voice. She pops up at the most unexpected times, and with some of the most random thoughts, inventions and suggestions. In business, I would describe her as my inner sounding board. For the sake of clarity, let's call her Carol. So, you see, Carol is really my best friend. She knows my every little idiosyncrasy, my strengths and weaknesses, my dreams and my aspirations.

When I was growing up, I would refer to Carol as my guardian angel. I wasn't being disrespectful, you understand, but when you're eleven or twelve it's nice to know someone is looking out for you, especially if school isn't the most awe-inspiring place that everyone else seems to think it is. Nowadays, Carol has developed into more of a trusted ally, one of the directors in my mental boardroom who offers advice and direction when called upon. She isn't infallible, but she does give me a different perspective when necessary and usually sees me through hard decisions or, as in my early days, difficult situations.

Do you believe in coincidence, chance happenings? I don't. I believe that you are where you are because it's in your stars. It has been mapped out in the universe. Yes, you have choices and, yes, you may take the odd detour, but, inevitably, if you're open to the world around you, you'll get the most out of it and eventually you'll get to where you want to be.

For me, I was always certain about at least three things in life. First, I knew some day I would die and, as death formed part of my life from a very early age, I'm okay with this thought (for the moment anyway). Second, you reap what you sow – those who work hard will enjoy the gains and, more importantly, appreciate the journey and the rewards. And third, although there is a book in most of us aching to be written, I've always believed that I would write at least one. I also knew the age at which I'd write it, and that was as far as my big plan went.

So, here Carol and I sit, wondering what exactly I want to write; hoping to dissipate any negatives thoughts, to erase the 'how' and 'why' and likelihood of writer's block.

Lesson one: Just do it!

Why is age so important to many of us – especially women? I'm in my forties and I think I don't look my age; I believe I'm at least ten years younger. Perhaps I'm in denial. After all, age is only dictated by a birth cert. However, lately I find myself reminiscing. I'm in the middle of a task or chore and my mind starts wandering back to something random, an incident or event in my past. Perhaps it's the onslaught of dementia or perhaps it's Carol reminding me about the passage of time and the precious gift that is life, and to 'live every day as if it were your last.' It's common knowledge that the second half of your life simply flies. But I never really believed it – until now. I feel I have been catapulted forward in time with full ferocity, as if I stepped into a time machine. In a blink, a chunk of my precious life has vanished.

I sometimes get so giddy and excited inside. I have so many plans that I could burst with enthusiasm. My only gripe is that I won't have enough time to fulfill my many ambitions for myself and for my family. Will I get to make that 'big difference' in the world that I believe I was born to make?

When I was young, my sister Marion gave me a poem called 'A Minute'. She used to keep a tiny, green, hardback notebook with her and in it she would scribble and sketch all day. I have kept it safely all these years as a memento of the time we spent growing up together. I suppose I should give it back to her some time soon.

> *A Minute*
> I have only just a minute,
> Only sixty seconds in it.
> Forced upon me, can't refuse it,
> Didn't seek it, didn't choose it.
> But it's up to me to use it.
> I must suffer if I lose it,
> Give account if I abuse it.
> Just a tiny little minute,
> But eternity is in it.
> **(author unknown)**

I already know that I'm behind schedule.

I had set my life goals over a decade ago and I'm about six years behind. How does someone whose work is all about timelines and deadlines manage to put her calendar out so far? Well, perhaps I should start by telling you a little bit about myself and maybe somewhere along the line we'll find the answer. First and foremost, I'm going to admit out loud for all to hear that I have always been a late developer. This doesn't mean I apply lateness to other parts of my life, like a philosophy. I'm always early for appointments and meetings, for everything really – at least in my business life. You only get one opportunity to make a first impression – and those first sixty seconds of introduction can make or break a deal. If you're running late, you become automatically flustered, you look unprofessional and you are already starting out on the back foot.

Being a late developer isn't obvious until after the fact. For example, I should have written this book six years ago; it was in my master plan after all. But perhaps it just wasn't the right time. I firmly believe that everything happens for a reason and, on reflection, so much has happened in the last six years – I've had a child; I've got married; I've set up my own business. In other words, I'm now ready!

I'm assuming you're a woman. If you're a man, I'm really hoping you're a 'metro man' as much of what I have to say in this book is touchy-feely and I don't make any apologies. Alongside the emotive and creative elements, you'll also find a good helping of common sense and commercial agility. These are not the traits of a convent girl who was told to be a nurse or marry well. I truly hope career guidance teachers have changed their perspective on life since I was at school.

Looking from the outside in, I'm an entrepreneur – someone who takes a certain amount of risk to realise a vision or a dream. The word 'entrepreneur' has been bandied about so much of late. It used to be special and I felt I was a member of a passionate and potentially powerful movement. Now everyone thinks they are an entrepreneur, but if you look more closely you'll see that this really isn't the case. For me, entrepreneurs build; they are 'architects of change'. They see something that others can't and they spend years, sometimes a lifetime, delivering on their vision to a market of naysayers (at first anyway). The trick is to ensure that your vision can be delivered in your lifetime, preferably before you retire, so you can hopefully reap the benefits.

Ask yourself this question – who inspires you, really inspires you? Put the book down and take a minute to think. If I was to stand in front of a room full of people and ask them that question, nine times out of ten I would hear – Richard Branson, Lord Sugar, Nelson Mandela and, if I'm lucky, Mother Teresa. Men take top poll position time and time again, with the more socially conscious perhaps citing the inspiring women of our time. To narrow it down, who in an Irish business context inspires you? Take a moment and think really hard. Not so easy, is it? Especially now that austerity rules.

A couple of years back you might have said Padraig O'Ceidigh, Aer Arann, but for the last number of years his business has lost millions on the back of a history of profit-making – does that make him yesterday's news? I don't think so. Let's face it, we Irish do tend to write off people pretty quickly. As a fickle nation, we love you one minute and lambast you the next. Then there's Brody Sweeney of O'Briens Sandwich Bars fame, who was always high up on the 'popular' businessman Richter Scale. But, alas, his Midas touch went AWOL, O'Briens went into liquidation and was taken over by Abrakebabra Investments. I'd mention the Quinns only it's far too depressing.

Then, take the familiar brand of Hughes & Hughes, the nation's favourite family booksellers. The chain went into receivership in early 2010 due to the downturn and ambitious expansion plans into the UK. I sat with Derek Hughes, founder of the book chain, as part of a Student Enterprise Awards judging panel the weekend he had to close the doors of his empire. I was totally amazed that this man, who had gone through so much in the preceding months, still turned up to offer his experience and support to young potential entrepreneurs. His honesty about where it had all gone wrong was like a breath of fresh air. On one hand, I wondered what hope I have, as a publisher, if someone with such ability and experience was stopped in his tracks?

Talking to Hughes helped me understand that I'm small, I'm agile and I can therefore adjust with the market and control my costs. I don't have an upward-only lease. I don't have hundreds of employees. I can change quickly. Lesson learned.

There are many successful, homegrown entrepreneurs around − it's just that good news doesn't seem to make the news. And media is a very powerful tool, which can influence a nation, sway opinion, and create positive and negative waves. Unfortunately, we all appear to be wallowing in a pool of pessimism and self-destruction.

The people I've mentioned are all true entrepreneurs because, through their unique visions, they have changed people's lives, brought employment, delivered returns to the Exchequer and given the country choice in terms of travel, reading, food and so on. They have made a difference and will do so again and again; such is the nature of an entrepreneur. But, hey, where are all the women in the equation? There has been much debate about women's contribution or otherwise to our recession. I am one of those female entrepreneurs who started out at the beginning of the big 'R' in mid-2006, oblivious to what was coming down the line. And, if I'm being really honest, it was only a year later in the summer of 2007 that my alarm bells started ringing and Carol, my inner voice, started waving her arms in frustration and disbelief....But I digress.

This book focuses on how women are viewed in the business world and, more importantly, how they perceive themselves. It's a book which will clearly show that each woman can be successful without selling her soul. It embraces the power of women in a '*Sex and the City* meets Forbes' way.

I have divided the book into twelve chapters, each representing a month of the year. Each opens with a quote from an inspiring, successful businesswoman who has been interviewed in *WMB* magazine − and there have been many. Each month also includes a thought based on WMB Publishing's company ethos. There are four core values that form WMB's identity. They act as guardians of my brand – Aspiring, Individual, Visionary and Passionate.

Success for me changes as my life progresses. It may be winning a business deal one day or watching my daughter perform at sports day the next. Survival is the new success in the times we live in and I firmly believe that, once the cloak of economic gloom has lifted – and, yes, it will happen – those who remain 'open for business' will become the inspirational leaders for our next generation of hopefuls. I firmly believe that our children are so influenced by what's around them. We, as adults and parents, have a responsibility to act responsibly around our youth. We need to be role models; we need to encourage and offer support and security.

At a time that has brought such uncertainty into people's lives, in a world that appears to be regressing, there comes a new realisation. Women need to take control of their lives and their destinies. They need to step up to the plate and they need to participate in order that generations to come will have a world worth waiting for.

Can you recall your first memories? One thing is probably certain – you believed you could be a princess, a magician, a pop star. And if you wanted to be a princess and a pop star, there was no doubt that you could be both.

When did you stop believing in yourself and your abilities? Was it when you were told by one of your parents that 'you can't do that' or by a teacher, perhaps, or by your boss? Children have a huge sense of self-belief; their imagination knows no boundaries. Now, let's bottle up that enthusiasm and sell it to ourselves ten, twenty or thirty years down the line.

Chapter 1

Just Do It!

'What starts small can have enormous impact on many.'
— Cathy Black, president of Hearst Magazines, interviewed in *WMB*, issue 18

Month: January
Thought: When you lose, don't lose the lesson.

A T THE RIPE AGE of seven I suddenly grew up – I learned that bad things can happen. And it wasn't until my late teens that I was able to turn something tragic into a more positive catalyst.

The day I heard about my father's death, I was at my best friend Deirdre's house. It was a normal sunny Sunday during the summer holidays and we had just celebrated her seventh birthday a couple of weeks before. Isn't it funny how, when we look back at the summers of our youth, they always seemed to be hot? Deirdre lived over her parents' pub, so our days involved plenty of crisps, fizzy drinks and fun – all the things I wasn't allowed at home. Anyway, there we were hand-in-hand, when her mum asked me to sit on her knee as she had something important to tell me.

She told me that my father had taken ill and was in hospital. I lost my focus on what she was saying as a deep anxiety took me over. I pulled away from her and ran all the way home. My mum was nowhere to be seen, but my aunt, who would play an important role in my life going forward, was at the sink peeling spuds. Anyone would have thought she was peelings onions as the tears ran down her face. I looked at her and I knew that my father was dead. Life was to change irrevocably and the little girl, the youngest of a family of eight, grew up in that moment.

Of course, there was no ordinary funeral to follow. My father, you see, was Chief of Staff of the Irish army, so they came in their droves from far and wide. He was buried in Glasnevin Cemetery in the state plot right opposite Daniel O'Connell. A privilege, I know, but there I stood, a young, frightened child, looking at a huge square plot where lots of men were buried. 'But how will you remember where he is,' whispered Carol. I didn't know the answer.

I have three vivid memories of that day. The first was that I was instructed not to cry. Imagine telling a child of seven who had just lost her daddy that she wasn't to cry, especially in front of the cameras! I remember approaching my father's open coffin and looking at him, barely able to reach above the casket stand. He lay still, pale and sombre in his uniform, his medals and brass buttons sparkling in the stained-glass light. I wanted to shake him, tell him to wake up, but I was quickly ushered away. My third memory was of President de Valera beckoning me over to his big car and taking me up on his knee. Even to a little girl, this gentle old man seemed so important, so strong, and yet he seemed to share in my sadness.

It was only when I turned twelve that I understood my father was never coming home. You see, Carol, that little voice inside me, who helped me cope all those years ago, had convinced me that Daddy was on a secret mission, working undercover, and that when I passed his open coffin on the day of the funeral he was really only in a deep sleep like Sleeping Beauty. But I was wrong.

So, I guess I learned from an early age that sad things happen to all of us and in order to cope you need to be strong and have a good guardian angel to watch over you. The loss of my father was hard. My life changed forever. But I lost two fathers on that day. My father worked such long hours and was travelling a lot, so Mum had an orderly to help in his absence, Tom. Tom was our 'Man Friday' and he drove me to and collected me from school each day. He was a part of my young life, but he too disappeared after my father died – perhaps they were on a secret mission together after all.

The dynamics of our household also altered as my remaining brothers pitched for the title of 'Man of the House', the two eldest brothers having long since left the nest. My mother was a very traditional woman. She had married at the age of nineteen and was deeply religious. Her ambitions were for her family, primarily for the boys. My sister and I didn't receive the same attention. One might wonder where I got my stubborn streak from, my drive and desire to be independent. Over the years it dawned on me – I'm my father's daughter in so many ways.

I had five brothers and two sisters. The firstborn, Bernadette, died twelve hours after she took her first breath. She would have led the family, but I guess it just wasn't to be. It must have been such a devastating time for my parents, particularly given the fact that, as Bernadette hadn't been baptised, she could not be buried in 'sacred ground'. Can you comprehend spending nine months preparing for your first birth only for your baby to be taken away with such little respect, in the name of 'religion'? To this day, I have no idea what happened to my big sister and it was obvious that it was a painful memory for my mother. She began producing children like rabbits from there on in: Damien, PJ, Michael and Paul, and then my father's other pride and joy, my beautiful sister Marion. Brendan came next and, finally, me. I'm not sure if I was a mistake because you would have thought, at that stage, there were enough mouths to feed. But I guess that the role of mother was an important one for a woman at that time, and still is. Given that the only contraception in those days was abstinence, well, I was an inevitable gift. And I was probably the reason why the double bed was soon to be replaced by two singles!

Apart from the eldest and youngest boy, my brothers followed in my father's footsteps and joined the army. At one stage, pressure was put on me to consider joining up. My brother Paul said, 'You would get a good university education and it wouldn't cost a penny.' Money was tight when my father passed away so this made perfect economic sense. 'You can even buy your way out of the army once you've completed your degree and served some time.' To me, this sounded like a prison sentence. You don't buy yourself out of the army – especially if you're the daughter of the Chief of Staff. The army becomes a part of your extended family – you never leave. I knew this from an early age and was to experience the unique lifelong relationship of family and army once again when Paul passed away a few years ago at the tragic age of just forty-nine.

On reflection, my childhood and teenage memories were good and I remember quite clearly the time that my entrepreneurial traits began to surface. One of our tasks as the girls in the family was the ironing. However, the boys were responsible for ironing their army shirts. Now, these had to be done to strict pristine standards. I quickly recognised an opportunity to earn some money. I charged 50 pence for each army shirt, which took 30 minutes to iron. You could buy quite a lot for 50 pence in those days and my little arrangement worked out quite well for all concerned – a win-win!

I wasn't that interested in school. I wasn't a troublemaker; I just wasn't that inspired. However, there was one girl in our class who was always top of the class. Roisín was prefect material. She was popular and talented to boot, a straight 'A' student as opposed to my dismal 'D' performances. She was a fantastic writer and her essays were always read out in class. I'd listen intently and think, 'How can she write like that?' I was really inspired by her talent but didn't have an ounce of confidence in my own abilities. Instead of listening in class, I'd spend hours lost in my own little world, with Carol happily keeping me company. You see, Carol loved to write poetry and doodle and she also had a fantastic imagination. We'd gaze out the gigantic convent windows, across the sea to Dalkey Island. All that separated me from this idyllic view was a grass verge. I was living in a poet's Mecca.

I wrote many poems both at school and at home from an early age. By the time I was sixteen, some had appeared in the national press. I managed to astound my teachers and my principal when one of my poems was published in the national teacher's magazine. I don't know what prompted me to submit it, but it was published for all to see. However, the theme was not exactly suited to an educated convent girl from the Loreto Order. It was entitled 'Suicide' and caused quite a stir at the time. In fact, my best friend Deirdre was interrogated at length by the hierarchy in the school as to the inspiration for such a piece. In other words, was Rosemary likely to top herself any time soon? This was probably when I started to become quite cynical about the school curriculum and the manner in which it was taught. I firmly believed that poetry and writing, in many cases, came from somewhere special. I thought that the author was purely the medium, the ink in the pen, so to speak. Obviously people are inspired by their experiences. Equally, there may be no rhyme or reason for writing something and therefore one should not try to over-analyse or box in the scribe. Was I a potential suicide risk or was I purely a medium? As I'm alive and well and by all accounts a happy-go-lucky kinda gal, I'm assuming the latter. However, I did give my teachers something to gossip about for quite a while, I'm sure!

It was probably when I started studying for my Leaving Cert. that it dawned on me that there was an inequity in my life. It wasn't obvious to me at first, but I began to look around me and see how some of my friends' fathers had already organised jobs for them in banks after their exams. Others had parents who'd spent the previous years helping them with their studies so that they would become doctors and surgeons, and follow in their footsteps. University was on the cards for quite a few of my classmates as they displayed above average grades. The chip on my shoulder began to show itself as it became clear that I had only myself to depend on. It was a chip that I quickly turned into a positive trait – I would sink or swim on my own merits. I would work for what I got in life and I wouldn't depend on anyone for anything. Lesson learned.

I believe you come across three types of people in life. There are those who rise above the pulpit, put themselves out there and take risks – I'll call these Type A. Type B are quite happy plodding through life until they get to the end. Then there's Type C – the misery streaks who moan about everything and everyone. The world owes them a living. You know who they are. I'm severely allergic to this type of person, but they're all around us. Their negativity stunts growth: their own growth and anyone who comes within an ass's roar of them. Their selfishness is contagious but the funny thing is they're survivors; they're the greatest con artists of our time. If they work, they do the bare minimum and quibble all the way to the bank. If they're out of work, it's not their fault and, by God, they're going to milk the system for every drop because, after all, they're owed it.

When I look at some of our more media-friendly entrepreneurs, I can't help but feel there's an important lesson to learn. Take, for instance, Lord Sugar. This is a man who came from very humble beginnings, leaving school at sixteen and four years later founding Amstrad. He has never looked back. Or look at Oprah Winfrey, who, despite an abusive and dysfunctional upbringing, excelled in school to later study media – the rest, as they say, being history. Similarly our own Bill Cullen, who was born into poverty and left school at thirteen to work in the local markets, later went on to make his millions with the Renault dealership. So, although there are successful people who are 'born with a silver spoon in their mouths', equally there are extremely successful entrepreneurs who are born hungry and turn this hunger to their advantage. I now know that the loss of my dad at a very young age moulded me into the person I am today: perhaps a Type A mixed with Type B, but never a Type C. It's good to remember that there'll always be someone worse off or better off than you – you make your own luck.

The one sure thing that all of us know in life is that it's going to end. So embrace it, feel it, discover it, uncover it. Don't just sit there miserable, making everyone around you miserable. Don't just think, 'What if?' but instead think, 'Why not?' Barack Obama being elected president was a historical moment in our lifetime on so many scales. Closer to home, watching as Mary Robinson was made the first female president of our country was a major landmark. Mary Robinson and her successor President Mary McAleese have inspired me on so many levels. These people are flesh and blood just like you and me. The difference, perhaps, is that they dared to dream and to believe in their abilities. They wanted to see change and be a part of that change. The spiritual leader Mahatma Gandhi put it most eloquently when he said: 'Be the change you want to see in the world.'

So don't make excuses – Just do it!

Chapter 2

The Glass Illusion

'The glass ceiling is definitely there, I mean you see it and it happens. You can't have a heart and say that everything is fair in life because it's not, period. But there are so many positives to being a woman and we have such an advantage today than at any time before.'
– Gina Gallo, Ernest & Julio Gallo, interviewed in *WMB*, issue 23

Month: February
Thought: Be careful what you wish for.

A
S ALICE PONDERED on what the world would be like through the looking glass, so, too, do women spend far too much time looking through potential glass barriers. If you think you can, or think you can't – you're probably right! I have always had a strong sense that thoughts are things. So, if you believe you are going to succeed, well, most likely you will.

I was in my thirties when I was first introduced to the term 'glass ceiling'. Up to that point, I had never heard it used, well not in my working life anyway. That is not to say that I hadn't experienced it – I just hadn't put a label on it or let it define my life in any way. At a bi-monthly board meeting in Mac Communications, the company I worked for at the time, my group CEO mentioned the term in passing and I asked what he meant by it. There was a spontaneous outburst of laughter from the ten-man board and, to this day, I cringe with embarrassment.

But let's look at this more closely. At the time I was a single woman in my thirties, in the position of managing director of a multimillion euro publishing business. Mac Communications was one of the most successful publishing corporations in Ireland at the time, with titles ranging from *Old Moore's Almanac* to *Discover Ireland*. We were the sales house for the *Sunday Times* and publishers of *Irish Medical News*. My chairman was the very successful, imposing and now defunct Seán Fitzpatrick, and some of the other directors were equally as colourful. So perhaps, on reflection, ignorance is bliss. I had reached the top of my profession at an early age and in a male-dominated business, and I was holding my own. I had no perception of failure or glass barriers. Up until that meeting, I had no idea what a glass ceiling was; I had just seen a goal and went for it.

Unfortunately, there are now so many terms that describe the invisible barriers which exist for women and, indeed, diverse groups in business. I don't put women within a diversity context, although organisations often do. A group that represents half our population cannot and should not be labeled with the tag 'diverse'. Let's just think about it for a moment: you're working on ground-level looking up at the floor above, which contains the boardroom and all management staff – the penthouse of your dreams. You're qualified, hard working, loyal and dedicated. You help your colleagues, you go that extra mile, you put the company first and you make sacrifices. But for some reason you never get invited upstairs. The longer you wait for your turn, the further away it seems to get. Then it dawns on you – you've got the brains but you also have the boobs. You're busted!

This is the experience of many of our young ambitious

women. Once they recognise they can't get past that glass ceiling, they leave and go in other directions. They may become successful entrepreneurs; they may become failed entrepreneurs. They may take time out to pursue more personal or life-orientated goals. But, at some point, a lot of talented women find out after years of toil that they don't have the right credentials for membership to the elite club of management – run by men, for men. Am I being too harsh? Let's look at the figures. According to *The Female FTSE Board Report 2010*:

> Overall, the percentage of women on FTSE 100 boards is 12.5%, showing a three year plateau. The number of companies with no female directors had decreased to 21 and the number of companies with more than one woman on the board has returned to the 2008 figure of 39. Only 13% of new appointments went to women. (Cranfield University School of Management 2010, p. 8)

An article in the *Sunday Times* outlined the attempts by the European Union to curb male domination of the boardroom with a move to require all publicly listed companies to have at least 40 per cent women on their boards. The message appears clear – adopt a new voluntary code or it may become compulsory. In the meantime, though, Ireland and many of her European friends lag embarrassingly behind France, Norway and Spain in such matters. Introducing quotas is a contentious issue, which traditionally I have been dead against. But when you see so few women in boardrooms and in the political arena, you wonder what it will take to change the status quo, and preferably in your lifetime. I ran a poll in *WMB* on this very topic and found that the majority of women were not in favour of quotas. Here are some of their thoughts:

Poll Question: Should quotas be introduced to create a better gender balance at board level?

'Absolutely not. Merit/suitability is more appropriate.'

'No. It could possibly lead to bias from male colleagues about the legitimacy and merit of the candidate.'

'I don't believe in quotas. Let us women encourage and facilitate more women in the workplace and in politics.'

'While I feel strongly that there should be inclusion, particularly at management level and on boards, to promote a sense of balance, representation and fair play, I believe that quotas won't be effective and in fact will prove divisive. Quotas will serve only to antagonise other participants who have earned their place at the table. Women should be represented on their merits in the natural order of business.'

'The best person for the job should be hired/elected not just because of their gender.'

'No to gender quotas. Where would it end – quotas for blondes?'

'I believe in a fair world the most qualified person should get the job – but unfortunately we don't live in a fair world and judgements are made based on gender, age, etc. all the time. I am not in favour of gender quotas. I would like to see more fairness and transparency in terms of hiring candidates as well as pay scales.'

Okay, so quotas aren't too popular. There is really only one conclusion to draw if you've come to realise that membership to your boardroom is closed – you're in the wrong working partnership and divorce is imminent. If you feel you have exhausted all possibilities of elevation in your current company, you need to get your sorry ass out of there before you lose your passion and, more importantly, your edge. You need to leave before it gets ugly. The right company culture is more important than the right salary. As you spend half your waking life working, you need to get this part of your life right. As well-known motivational guru

Jack Black of MindStore explains, you need to balance your wheel of life. If it's not balanced, you are going to have a very rocky road ahead of you. But more about that later (see Chapter 3).

Several years ago, two professors from Exeter University discovered a worrying trend which they labelled the 'glass cliff'. Imagine, if you will, standing at the edge of the world knowing that if you take another step you'll fall into oblivion. Research undertaken by our two professors showed that, once women had managed to break through the glass ceiling, their experiences differed from their male counterparts. So, there you are, having celebrated your recent promotion, no doubt with a bottle or two of pink champagne; you get down to the job in hand with positive enthusiasm only to find that you've inherited a poisoned chalice. This precarious new situation that you find yourself in comes with a high risk of failure and is usually the result of poor company management – a business in crisis – or lack of support and resources to do the job. Now the latter point doesn't sit well with me, as one would assume that you would be in a position to improve systems and resources since, after all, you are the boss. But if shareholders don't want to re-invest and since cash is the bloodline of any business, well, you'll be dead in the water in no time. The expression 'Be careful what you wish for' comes to mind.

During my career, I moved jobs quite a bit. At the time, I thought I was unlucky but, on reflection, I realise that I had one of the best apprenticeships a girl could ask for. There seemed to be two paths open to me on leaving school – one led to university and the other to a good job, which at the time was in the bank or the civil service (yes, a job for life!). Although I had been accepted into a media studies course at a Dublin university, the funding did not materialise for this rather new discipline and I was left high and dry. I decided to do the shortest secretarial course I could find, as I was keen to start earning a living. The *Irish Times* as a brand was synonymous with respectability and, as chance would have it, their new training division was running a six-week intensive secretarial course. I learned everything from speed typing to shorthand. Armed with these new tools, I joined the workforce, and, over a few short years, immersed myself in various tasks from debt collecting to marketing timeshares. However, I wanted more from life and decided to sell my one true possession – my beautiful Blue Fiat 127 – and head for Europe. As I was just about to leave, a position in Bord Scannán na hÉireann (the Irish Film Board) came up. I was nineteen and knew that these opportunities didn't happen every day. I put off my travel plans to a later date and embraced the opportunity.

Many people believe the film business is glamorous and, to an extent, I'm sure it is. However, we were working primarily in the business of grant aiding the Irish industry, which at the time had talent in abundance but little by way of financial aid and international recognition. I have both good and bad memories of my time at Bord Scannán na hÉireann. Yes, I got to read scripts, in my own time. Yes, I got to visit film locations, even if I was only the chauffeur. I even met some great actors like Bob Hoskins, Brenda Fricker and the beautiful Alison Doody. While I was taking notes at a board meeting one day, flowers were delivered for me. They were from Ros Hubbard of Hubbard Casting (who has discovered the likes of Jonathan Rhys Meyers, Colin Farrell and Kate Winslet) to thank me for a 'good deed' I had done. It was probably one of the proudest memories in my young life as the board members around the table nodded in affirmation.

I give credit to my then boss for setting me on the right path. He was one of my earliest mentors, but at the time I totally didn't appreciate the fact. While I thought he was moody, opinionated and arrogant, he also displayed oodles of patience and understanding. As I mentioned earlier, I was a bit of a dreamer in school but he saw someone with promise and was determined to drag me screaming from an average to an ambitious young lady.

His attention to detail when communicating was second to none and he drove this home to me, day in and day out. Bord Scannán na hÉireann was unfortunately closed in 1987. I left there a very different individual – I was no longer the naïve school leaver, but a creative, confident young woman who was in love with all things media related.

I remained on this media-related path with a stint working as a production assistant on the film *Taffin*, working out of Ardmore Studios. I still have the signed photo from Pierce Brosnan. I then moved to the state broadcasting agency, RTÉ, to work in their Film Department. I recall being asked how I had managed to secure a job at RTÉ as I must have known someone. My response was simple – I just applied! I am amazed at the amount of people I come across who are miserable in their current jobs. But when I ask them to tell me what company they would rather work for, they look slightly puzzled. Humour me with this simple exercise – if you're in a job that you don't like, take out a notepad and jot down the top five companies where you'd rather work. They may come easily, or you may need to take some time out to think about it. Now, once you've identified them, write their individual merits beside each. Is it their perceived company culture that attracts? Are they led by a visionary and inspirational entrepreneur? Are they the best in their field? Now ask yourself, what have you got to offer them? Have you the right qualifications, the experience, the drive? I'm guessing you do and all that's missing is for you to take that first step. As an employer, I will always look over those CVs that I have on file first when filling a post. These candidates have already shown me that they are interested in my company. It also saves on advertising, recruitment agency costs and my time. So introduce yourself to the HR head. Connect on LinkedIn or a similar social networking site. It's all about being in the right place at the right time. I applied to RTÉ and my CV happened to land on the desk of a total stranger with the power to make it happen. Lesson learned!

Unfortunately working for RTÉ wasn't what I had envisaged. On reflection, there were many glass barriers – I just didn't stop to think about them. It was quite an antiquated environment. For instance, I had to refer to my boss as 'Mr', whereas my male colleagues could address him by his first name. Actually, most of the managers around me were male. The marriage ban, after all, had only been lifted a decade before. I was an outsider when I joined RTÉ. I had come in without any connections, with no preconceived notions. I was hardworking, obliging and enthusiastic. I wasn't tainted by office politics and my ambitions for life were fresh and idealistic. I learned many things in my early days there. I learned that I couldn't change a light bulb when it blew because that was someone else's job; I had to apply in triplicate for a replacement biro; I was never to stay late as I would 'rock the boat'; and there was most definitely a two-tier system in operation – a top tier for the men and a lower tier for the women (with a glass pane in between).

I knew if I stayed that I would lose my edge, my ambition to succeed. I applied for the position of trainee producer in TV and, after a long and challenging interview process, I was put on a panel. This was quite a coup at the time, but it soon dawned on me that I could be waiting on the panel for a year or more. Having talked to a couple of people within the organisation, I decided that I had the perfect opportunity to satisfy those travel cravings. When the opportunity comes your way to travel, you need to take it as it may not come again. I was a contract employee, one of many. When I was called off the panel to take up my training, I would return from my travels.

I landed in the US on a holiday visa and headed for Newport, Rhode Island with a friend. The first night we landed, I met a very handsome actor who was working as a caretaker in one of the famous mansions. Did I mention that he was a failed actor? It didn't really matter. Newport is the town where Jacqueline Lee

Bouvair married John F. Kennedy in their summer mansion, Hammersmith Farm. It is simply a beautiful town by the sea, dotted with quaint shops, a marina and hundreds of colourful wooden houses. However, I was immediately struck by the division between rich and poor; black and white. I used to pass a shopfront window each morning on my way to work, which was covered in missing persons posters. I was struck by the fact that the majority were young black kids. A common practice was to put a missing person's picture on a milk carton – it was all so new to me and somewhat macabre.

I worked as a waitress in a restaurant that was famous for its clam chowder and people would travel far and wide to savour the taste – they never knew it came from a tin! One of the first tips I got was a $50 bill, such a big amount. The customer had made me promise that I'd go and visit the mansions with the money – but I found better uses for it! My six weeks came and went as I fell in love with Newport, the freedom of working in a constant holiday atmosphere and in a town where you didn't need insurance to drive your car. We moved digs into a better part of town and on some occasions there were as many as ten of us sleeping in two rooms. I got used to sharing a small single bed with two others as we fought over who could sleep closest to a small fan which was the only form of air conditioning in our attic abode.

Once autumn arrived, however, living in Newport was a totally different experience. Jobs were harder to come by as the tourist trade dried up. Money was always a problem and we scrimped and scraped for the rent. We were very friendly with a gang of Basque guys who were in Newport to play jai alai – a variety of Basque Pelota. There seemed to be one big, continuous party going on at their house and a friend of mine started dating one of them quite seriously. I remember, when it was really cold, going out in their car and borrowing (long term) some firewood from one of our neighbour's front yards. I was so afraid of being caught and deported as a thief, but it was only done in jest and perhaps out of necessity.

Eventually, I got homesick. I was tired of worrying where the rent money would come from and it was getting really cold. My aunt in Boston came to the rescue and paid for my trip home to Ireland. I left the US knowing that it was one of the best life experiences I could have wished for. I also realised how naïve I had been at times and that someone was definitely looking out for me.

I was fortunate to be able to return to RTÉ on contract and was offered a job in Millennium Radio as a production assistant. (I still remained on the panel for trainee TV producer.) This was my first taste of radio and I loved it. The station was set up to celebrate Dublin's Millennium and was situated at the GPO Arcade on the north side of the Liffey. It was a new experience for this south-side gal, but I soon got to love the banter of the vendors selling their wares on Moore Street. We had coffee mornings regularly, which attracted all sorts of listeners to the station for a cuppa. For the most part, my job was to keep the public happy, the coffee flowing and the requests coming. I stood in reception and directly behind me was the DJ's glass booth. For a young, impressionable girl, it was a fantastic place to work and I enjoyed every minute of it. It involved listening to music all day, dealing with all manner of character, and, of course, I had an excellent view of some rather handsome DJs! However, the station had a lifespan of one year and once the celebrations were over it was defunct. Many of those employed at Millennium Radio still remain within media – Scott Williams (102fm), Andrew Hanlon (heads up news at TV3) and Robbie Irwin (sports presenter at RTÉ). I returned once again to the Film Department at RTÉ and was immediately struck by how time had stood still for those colleagues who I had left behind. My stay this time was to be short-lived.

The year was 1989: the Berlin Wall had crumbled and East and

West were reunited; the US had invaded Panama; the Exxon Valdez oil spill, one of the most devastating human-caused environmental disasters, unfolded in Alaska; and Soviet forces withdrew from Afghanistan. The same year, the airwaves opened up to competition and Ireland saw the launch of Century Radio – the third national and independently run station. It was a big event for a small country with a population at the time of just 3.5 million.

I was offered a position as production assistant in the News Department in Century Radio and was on the move again. I really didn't want to languish in the Film Department at RTÉ and the road to being a producer seemed too long. I did know one thing for certain though: when I handed in my notice the second time around, I was closing the door to a career in RTÉ forever. At the time, Century were trying to poach leading RTÉ presenters and rumour had it that Gay Byrne was offered close to a cool million to make the move. However, many of their attempts failed as they searched for their golden voice of independence. I recall at the time that my mother was furious with my decision. I was moving from a stable employer to a new venture – some habits die hard! However, once you work in radio it gets into your bloodstream and anything else just isn't as exciting. Century was calling and I was more than happy to take up the new challenge.

During my time there, I worked primarily in three areas – the newsroom, on a current affairs programme and in promotions. The station was doomed from the outset as it was a common belief that the founders were really only interested in making a quick buck and weren't necessarily in it for the long haul. There was great difficulty with transmission services. At the time, RTÉ were providing the masts for Century and I'm sure the relationship must have been a fraught one!

Probably one of the bigger names to cross over from RTÉ to Century at the time was Marty Whelan. I recall he was quite the gentleman and always had a family photo on his desk and a positive disposition. However, a lot rested on his shoulders as the station grappled for loyal listeners. In the two years that I was there, I had at least three or four chief executives and numerous station managers. It meant the pressure was always on to be good at your job, to get noticed. I moved to Current Affairs and finally took up a post in the Promotions Department. I had found my niche. I primarily planned competitions, outside broadcasts and the like. My manager was a young English lass who was a total stranger to Ireland and our culture. However, at this stage the station was two years into broadcasting and was losing a fortune. We still had issues with transmission and couldn't attract big names. My manager didn't hang around for long as cutbacks were made, and yet another new station manager was intro-duced. I remained working in Promotions and had a small team working with me. It was my first taste of middle management, which wasn't so much offered to me, but I was in the right place at the right time. I worked extremely long hours and travelled the length and breadth of the country promoting Century. My job was so varied that you probably couldn't write a job descrip-tion. You would find our great 40ft outside broadcast unit at anything from the Tall Ships Festival in Cobh to Limerick's Main Street outside Supermacs.

There are a number of things that I took away from my experience at Century. I was so lucky to have worked with such a creative team of individuals. I'd learned that you are only as good as your last gig, no one is indispensable and, finally, that you make your own opportunities. Century closed down in November 1991, having lost millions. We didn't get much notice of this beforehand, but the rumours had been rife for weeks. My three colleagues, with whom I also lived, and I lost our jobs on the same day. Although we were quite broke, we managed to drown our sorrows on sympathy and goodwill that night. I had to return my beautifully branded jeep and my out-sized mobile phone. The bubble had burst, the dream was over and all our hard work was in vain.

Suddenly I was penniless and possibly looking at moving back home for the first time in years. With Christmas looming, I became a dole queue statistic like so many others. I remember my friend's dad won a turkey in a golf outing and donated it to us for Christmas dinner. It was one of those rare moments when you experience the true wealth of someone's generosity. We even managed to buy a little re-potable Christmas tree, which we decorated with popcorn. Yes, we may have been broke but we still had the Christmas spirit.

Reality did hit home, though, as jobs were hard to come by and were non-existent in our area of expertise. I eventually received some redundancy and tax back and, with this, I, together with the former head of engineering at Century, purchased some broadcasting equipment at the right price from the liquidated stock. Together, we spent the next year compiling a feasibility study on the merits of operating an outside broadcast unit for the various independent stations around the country. Although our business plan was comprehensive and we managed to secure some serious funding commitments, we got cold feet before launch. A postal and banking strike intervened and we looked to pastures new. On reflection, this was my first potential taste of entrepreneurship and, although I had put almost a year of sweat and toil into the project without any payment or immediate results, I knew the experience wouldn't be lost.

Chapter 3

The Power of the Notebook

'The greatest gift in life is the ability to think great thoughts and have the strength to take action so that those thoughts become reality in this wonderful and abundant world.'

— Jack Black, founder of MindStore; speaker at the inaugural
WMB Conference & Awards, 2007

Month: March
Thought: Believe

I LIVE BY TWO MANTRAS: 'What goes around, comes around' and 'If you can dream it, you can do it.' The latter can be attributed to the innovator Walt Disney and it encompasses all that is magical and wonderful about making your dreams come true. I have already admitted that I am a late developer. But if time dictates to us too much, and we are too busy thinking about what has already passed or about that which is yet to come, we may forget to live in the here and now.

When I was very young, I remember often waking during the night and feeling so inspired to write. I used to have a small notebook and pencil beside my bed and can vividly remember 'the pen taking over' as I wrote prose and verse in the dark of night, not wishing to wake my older sister. I used to think it odd at the time as I'd no idea where all the words were coming from. I came to the conclusion that I was the mere vehicle through which someone else was writing – a medium of sorts.

Three decades later, I still have a notebook beside my bed. I also have one in my handbag as I am constantly getting 'light bulb' moments. My little pink book is full of names, notions and some not-too-clever thoughts. Many of my ideas are so farfetched that it's too embarrassing to even mention them. But I can safely say that this notebook is evidence that inside me there's a writer and inventor dying to break out. I usually use my husband as a sounding board for my latest 'must have' gadget or notion. A recent idea of mine was that it would be cool to have a website for anything to do with funerals, from coffin choice to obituary writing. I thought, 'Well, we all have to die sooner or later!' Then I thought of a hundred reasons why I shouldn't do it. Probably high up the scale would be the challenge of getting the long-established funeral homes cartel on side. While you could develop all the other parts of what would be quite a unique site, they could end up screwing you on the most important element – the coffin.

Another lightbulb moment came about as I was rushing to a meeting on St Stephen's Green. I wanted to apply some lipper (yes, in public) and had no mirror. So I thought, 'Gosh, wouldn't it be cool to have a mirror app on my iPhone!' My husband was more enthused about this idea. However, on further examination, we realised that a company had already spent a considerable amount of lolly researching this one.

Another inspiration relates to something I came across when I lived in the US. Over there, when we ironed, we had a simple plastic hook that attached to the top of the door on which you could hang your ironed shirts, etc. This simple device was ingenious. Anyone who irons knows that the backs of chairs usually get cluttered with bits and bobs as you work through your load of freshly washed, creased laundry. Wouldn't it be so much easier to have one hoop to accommodate everything? Alas, I found out that this little number does exist in Ireland; it's just hard to get your hands on it.

I'm constantly thinking of angles on how to improve the way we do things, the way we work, the way we engage. I believe in the Thomas Edison approach to ideas. According to Edison, 'To have a great idea, have a lot of them.' Over a decade ago I was exposed to a concept that focused my aspirations and thinking more clearly – a combination of mental programming mixed in with meditation. My then employer had heard of a motivator and business coach gaining popularity in Ireland and sent me along to an event as the token skeptic. The course was called 'MindStore for Business' and it was presented by Jack Black, the coaching guru (as opposed to the actor). I left the two-day session somewhat confused and not at all convinced. I just didn't really 'get it'. Not one to be deterred, though, I returned for a second helping to find that, this time, I totally got it. MindStore (www.mindstore.com) is based on easy-to-learn tools and techniques that deliver extraordinary performance. The approach is gleaned from Black's work with world champion athletes, entrepreneurs and business leaders. Fundamentally, the programmes are based around five characteristics of excellence in individual and team performance, which are: the ability to maximise personal energy levels; adoption of a profound, positive and 'can do' attitude; the commitment to achieve inspirational goals and targets; the integration of whole-brain thinking, leading to outstanding problem solving, creativity and innovation; and, finally, leveraging emotional intelligence. Basically, Jack Black gave me the tools to focus on my desires, which included a combination of grounding, soul searching, thought filtration and programming. But most important for me was the emphasis on goal setting.

Tell me, do you have goals? I'm talking more about life goals than specific project objectives here. I'm hoping you have and the fact that you've picked up this book would imply that you're open to learning about someone else's experiences. Okay, so you have a goal or goals. What MindStore taught me was to actually commit those goals to paper and revert to them consistently. I can say, with confidence and conviction, that you will realise your ambitions by taking this first simple step. Of course, there are many ways in which to maximise your potential, from practising visualisation to practising meditation. I'd like you to humour me by taking out your notebook and committing five goals to paper. Be brave and bold. Think big. This is exactly what I did and, over time, I reached my goals. Once I prioritised them, they were realised. Lesson learned.

Through MindStore for Business and for Life, I was able to channel my natural positive energy towards realising my goals, appreciate how far I had travelled in my short life and be able to recognise an opportunity when it came knocking. The course allowed time for soul searching and re-evaluation. I looked at all aspects of my life to see which areas needed more attention. One of the exercises involved evaluating yourself out of a score of ten on various aspects of your life – your work, your family relationships, your health, your spiritual side, and so on. It's a simple exercise and one that quickly throws up your weaknesses and strengths to give you some clear direction. In one of our exercises, I remember we had to set goals. Your immediate instinct might be to set realistic goals, but Jack Black encourages you to set ambitious goals. Whereas I would have previously said, 'I'd like to travel to Cuba,' I was now saying, 'I'd like to travel the world' (and, no, I haven't prioritised this goal as yet). Although I would have previously said, 'I'd like to be a director,' I was now saying, 'I'd like to be a managing director.' I think you get the idea. To this day, the many MindStore programmes that I have participated in have helped enormously in my career and my outlook on life. If I feel I need to refocus or if I'm going through a particularly challenging phase, I tend to revisit the programme and take a repeat course.

MindStore is not for everyone, but if it works for you, you'll realise that there are no boundaries, only new horizons. Sometimes when I'm doing my cashflow projections, instead of being too realistic, I set my targets that bit higher. It works. You stretch yourself and soon you realise that there's a bit more elasticity than you previously thought.

My career really started to take off when I embraced the MindStore leadership methods. At the time I was editor of a number of magazine titles. Now, you're probably wondering how I jumped from being an unemployed radio junkie to being a magazine editor, but the world works in mysterious ways.

To continue where I left off in the previous chapter, after being let go from Century, I had applied to a number of agencies for work. I got a call to see a lady about an editorial job in a new free ads newspaper. This was a departure for me as I really didn't have any print experience, but I went along to the interview. After two meetings and a lot of chatting, I'm convinced I got the job based on my admittance to being an utter shopaholic. As my role would be to compare prices of various products and services of interest to the general public, my honesty and passion for purchasing sealed the deal and I started my new role as editor of *Dandelion* (named after the Dandelion Market which was located off St Stephen's Green in the 1970s).

We were in direct competition with the free ads newspaper *Buy & Sell* and I was primarily working with an American and English management team. In fact, I soon discovered that I was working for the second-generation American media mogul Ralph Ingersoll, who at the time also owned half of the *Irish Press*, de Valera owning the balance. Ingersoll would visit the office on occasion and it was always a tense time. I was still young, inexperienced and out of my comfort zone. I had recognised quite early on that the publishers wanted a face for the paper, and a local Irish girl seemed to fit the bill. Ingersoll took a keen interest in the project and even found time out of his hectic schedule to teach me various editing skills. Ingersoll worked quite long hours, as was the American way, so it was not unusual for me to work twelve-hour days, which stretched to seventeen hours when he was around. Lunch breaks were a rarity and we often worked late into the night. I thought it was all rather counterproductive and, although I pitched in, I didn't always adhere to the heavy work regime.

I remember on one April Fool's Day my manager played a rather mean trick on me. Ingersoll owned an island in the Caribbean and, from time to time, he would summon key personnel to meetings with him there. On this particular weekend, I was really excited as my brother was coming home from Spain to visit and I hadn't seen him in over ten years. However, I got a call from Ingersoll to tell me that there was a ticket waiting at the airport as he wanted to meet to talk about the editorial schedule immediately. I was devastated and, after much nail biting, declined his offer. No one declined an Ingersoll request. I was left to stew for hours before I was told it was all one big April Fool's joke. How my manager managed to rope him into it, I'll never know, as I wouldn't have put 'strong sense of humour' as one of his endearing traits! I gained lots of experience and wrote many features during my time at *Dandelion*. However, with the closure of the *Irish Press* in the mid-nineties, Ingersoll exited with *Dandelion* in tow, and I was left hunting for a job once again.

I now had a portfolio, good writing skills and sound research techniques. I applied to the *Irish Independent* for freelance work and, within days, had my first assignment to write an article on 'how to win your way to the World Cup'. The year was 1995. I remember thinking 'But I don't know anything about rugby!' After two days of intense research, some rusty shorthand notes and a lot of coffee, I produced my first real national assignment. It was published in its entirety and took up three quarters of a page – I was on my way! I continued to freelance and my portfolio grew. However, anyone in the game knows that the worst part about freelancing, apart from the isolation, is getting paid. I waited sometimes three months for a cheque to arrive in the post for an assignment. I lived hand to mouth, all the while turning out some great copy. There just had to be a better way to earn a living.

Opportunity knocked when I got an interview at a local publishing house, Mac Communications. It was one of the main magazine publishers at the time with a lively sales floor and design, production, editorial and administrative areas. I was interviewed by the General Manager Una O'Hare and secured a position as editor of *Visitor* magazine. It was a contract position for six months and I embraced it with open arms. *Visitor* was the official Aer Rianta airport magazine and enjoyed a large circulation and healthy advertising. I rose to the task, which involved agreeing editorial content, commissioning and writing articles, sub-editing, managing the advertising sales and overseeing proofing, print and distribution. It was like a mini company and I loved it. I soon took on editorial responsibility for other titles. Over the following months, I carved a niche for myself as my confidence grew. It wasn't long before I was running the production department.

Una was a fair and hardworking boss who was happy to give me the reins and let me get on with the task in hand. I really enjoyed my new role, which had literally started out as one single assignment. Unfortunately, Una moved on to pastures new and I had a new boss to answer to. I decided that, as he was the new kid on the block, I had the advantage for the time being. I learned so much when my new boss came on board. He was an animal when it came to sales and had a great commercial eye. With a background in newspapers, he brought many opportunities to the company. We each had very different working styles and we locked heads on more than one occasion. But we also respected one another's strengths and probably understood one another's limitations. Together, we secured many tenders, and with every new contract came more work and increased responsibility.

I was in the thick of my career at this stage and long hours were the norm. There were plenty of business opportunities in the nineties and we took on some serious titles, but we also lost a few. It seemed to me that, as one area of the business did well, another suffered. It was all about getting the balance right and it was at this exact time that I was introduced to Jack Black and MindStore. My life started changing at an accelerated pace.

MindStore had me committing my goals to paper for the first time in a long time. Looking back on my goals at the time, I can remember my top seven goals more readily than the remaining twenty-three. In total you had to commit thirty goals to paper and Black would reiterate that, with the achievement of your first seven, the others would automatically materialise! I wanted to be a director at Mac; I wanted to buy the car of my dreams; I wanted to write a book; I wanted to be more health conscious; I wanted to meet Mr Right; I wanted to buy a house; and I wanted to be happy. Within months of setting the goals and being totally in the MindStore zone, I was made editorial director at Mac. With my increased package I was able to buy a house within the year. It was, for all intents and purposes, a bit of a two-bedroomed cowshed. But I loved it dearly. I had big plans for it. Although my family and friends thought I was nuts, I saw something in that space that no one else could – potential.

Within two years of being introduced to MindStore, I watched as one managing director moved up within the company and another took his place. My new boss was a very different individual and had a great passion for radio, not publishing. It wasn't long before he got itchy feet. It dawned on me that, in the past five years, Mac had had three managing directors. Each had used the company as a stepping stone to bigger opportunities. I decided it was time for me to make my move. I loved publishing and was able to manage all aspects, from the creative to the commercial. I had the support of my colleagues and also my financial director. I pitched myself for the post of managing director and was eventually given the reins. It took seven years and plenty of professional and personal investment to reach this level.

Of course, as I had already committed new goals to paper, this was pre-destined. With another MindStore course completed, came more ambitious goals. I had crossed 'Become a director' off my list and replaced it with 'Become a managing director.' I also had replaced my other important goal, 'Buy a house', with 'Build a home'. Lastly, within months of becoming the managing director, I bought the car of my dreams, a Mercedes convertible, which I drive to this very day.

Remember that 'thoughts are things.' As I thought my goals, dreamed my goals and planned my goals, they became a reality. I had reached the top of the ladder. I could go no further and was more than aware that I could easily fall back down to the bottom rung. So I made hay while the sun shone. With no dependants, I was able to take greater personal risks. I decided to turn my two-bedroom cowshed into a home. I secured a mortgage and engaged the services of the first woman to graduate as an architect under the watchful eye of none other than Duncan Stewart. She had fantastic taste to match my expensive taste and we got on like a house on fire. I decided from the outset that I wanted my friend's brother to build the house. He was from my home town, he was great at what he did and I knew he'd watch my back. It took a year to get both planning permission and the builder to commit. I moved in with my sister, who lived around the corner, for the duration of the build, which took exactly four months from demolition to completion. I was on site at 7.30 every morning and each evening after work. When I wasn't working, I was reading anything to do with home interiors (and exteriors). It was the most exciting project I had ever undertaken and the team were fun to work with and talented to boot. When it was finished it was the most beautiful light-filled two-storey space I could imagine. I had not only realised another goal but I had added considerable worth to my hitherto broken-down patch of land. I had become a millionaire – on paper at least!

There was also something uncanny about the valuation put on my new home. One of the books that Jack Black had previously recommended was *Think and Grow Rich* by Napolean Hill. In fact, Jack recommended a whole series of wonderful books, from *The Power of Your Subconscious Mind* by Dr Joseph Murphy to Eckhart Tolle's *The Power of Now*. If you can get your hands on Hill's book, go to Chapter 2. Here you will find a six-step plan to turn your desire for riches into its financial equivalent. I had figured out that, if I had a million euro, I wouldn't have to worry too much about money thereafter. According to Hill you have to:

> Write out a clear, concise statement of the amount of money you intend to acquire, name the time limit for its acquisition, state what you intend to give in return for the money, and describe clearly the plan through which you intend to accumulate it. Read your written statement aloud, twice daily, once just before retiring at night, and once after rising in the morning. As you read – see and feel and believe yourself already in possession of the money. (p. 42)

The amount I wrote down on my piece of paper was one million euro. In return, I would work really hard to accumulate it. The penny dropped when I got the valuation on my new home; I had acquired my desire – it just wasn't in the manner I had originally expected.

Life for me was moving at an incredible rate. However, work was demanding and, indeed, stressful. We had some major titles under our belts and our portfolio was diverse – anything from sales representation for the *Sunday Times* to a full publishing service for Tourism Ireland titles. However, much of our contract publishing was, by its very nature, for defined periods. I already knew that the *Sunday Times* was setting up its own in-house sales force and our exit strategy had already been agreed. There were other challenges as well. The year 2000 saw a ban on all cigarette print advertising, which crippled revenues on certain titles. It was nearly impossible to replace this lost revenue. There was always another tender to complete, and titles were lost and gained as we strove for balance and profitability.

I also felt quite vulnerable at the boardroom table. There were three accountants present and a number of other experienced heavy hitters. Although I fought my battles hard and knew the world of publishing inside out, I felt I was weak, especially in the area of finance. The Financial Director had been with the company for years and always discussed the budget in detail, whereas I could only talk broad strokes, targets, goals. He was old school and preferred pencil and paper. If I needed figures, I would have to wait for them. Patience was never one of my virtues, so I decided to take action. I looked at various courses available and identified a Diploma in Applied Finance as the best option.

Out of a class of twenty-four, there were only a few women. I was probably in the bottom four of the class when it came to any kind of accountancy experience. I had some serious catching up to do but I had made a commitment and I wasn't going to fail. Fortunately, we were all divided into project teams and I met some amazingly talented individuals who were more than happy to drag me up to speed. I knew I had to work twice as hard as everyone else and study twice as long. Once again, I locked myself away and closed myself off to family and friends in a bid to better myself. At the end of a long year, after much sweat and sometimes tears, I graduated with top marks (but, then again, so did everyone else). It was time to put what I learned into action.

I had realised one main motivation during my studies. I wanted to own and build something, rather than just contribute to it. Now, I need to make it clear. I was being paid a very fair salary and pension for a job I loved. But I believed that these were the best years of my life and that I was laying the foundations for what was yet to come. I wanted to know I was creating wealth and value for me as well as for shareholders. I knew that my predecessor had shares and felt that for me to be denied shares was a double standard, since I was doing the same job.

I had a number of conversations with my direct group boss. This led to a number of conversations with my chairman. But we were talking from different poles. I wanted to be part of something that I had part ownership of, whereas he was putting the focus on material matters. I knew he was just marking my card and that I would never get a shareholding. It was time for me to move on. It was time for me to invest in me.

My time at Mac is now a distant memory, but it was a pivotal point in my career. I worked with some talented individuals and also with some troublemakers. I realised that when you become managing director, you have to shoulder a lot of the burden on your own. In the process, you automatically distance yourself from those colleagues who you once worked with side-by-side. I learned that my decisions and those of the board would influence the livelihoods of many. Sometimes it was hard to take the personal out of it; sometimes I had no choice. It can be lonely when you have few sounding boards.

However, if a company culture isn't your culture, you need to reassess your needs and desires. I had learned all I was going to learn at Mac. I had gained all I was going to gain. I no longer saw the bigger picture because I would always be on the outside looking in – an important, albeit dispensable, employee but never the influential shareholder.

Chapter 4

From Boardroom to Bedroom

'I'm very direct and I don't think that you should beat around the bush. It's the right way of doing business – open and direct.'

Michelle Mone, founder of MJM International and the Ultimo lingerie brand; interviewed in *WMB*, issue 20

Month: April
Thought: Never give up.

T HE ROLE OF A PERSONAL ASSISTANT should never be under-estimated. Having a good PA allows you to spread yourself across a lot more work without spreading yourself too thin. One of the sacrifices I made when I gave up my 'permanent, pensionable job' for the somewhat precarious life of an entrepreneur was that I had to acknowledge that my PA was not in a position to come along with me as she had other commitments within the organisation. Julie was terrific. She organised the office and organised my life at Mac. She had previously worked for a Japanese firm and, get this, in her eigtheen years of service, she had rarely missed a day! I knew I was on to a good thing when I interviewed her. Now, Julie and I were opposites in some aspects and it was fun getting to know one another. She was highly organised, whereas I tended to fly by the seat of my pants (and I still do). At first she appeared straitlaced but I soon discovered this was not the case. She dressed meticulously, wore little or no make-up and had a dry sense of humour. I invariably showed a bit of cleavage, wore a healthy helping of lipper and had a gregarious disposition. But somehow we bonded and, over time, gained considerable respect for and trust in each other. However, Julie was like a dog with a bone when she had a mission to accomplish and she made my love life – or lack thereof – her number one priority.

A woman totally devoted to her husband, Julie couldn't understand why I hadn't been snapped up years ago. Yes, I had received a number of proposals, but for some reason I thought I had plenty of time for marriage and motherhood. How wrong I was! I was definitely going though a dry spell after my last disastrous break-up. In fact, I had my healing process down to a fine art by this stage – I just threw myself into my work and the local gym became my new best friend. It's strange that, no matter how many times your heart is broken, you still hold out hope that Mr Right will come along. I still had hope, despite the fact that I had my fair share of dating Mr Wrongs and had learned some valuable lessons about Mr Maybe. Women who are on top of their game, ambitious, driven, independent and confident can bring out the worst in a guy. I learned this valuable lesson from my continental ex.

Mr European was a good-looking guy who had totally adopted the Irish way of life, including the accent. We had dated for a couple of years in my late teens and, more than a decade later, we had begun seeing each other again. I thought that this was fate and embraced the moment. However, there were a few, dare I say, serious problems with our relationship, which basically came down to the two m's – monogamy and money. I'd always had a problem staying faithful to him and, on reflection, I think I was either afraid of commitment or he just wasn't the one. However, it was a conversation with one of his best friends that put an end to any potential happily-ever-after. Seemingly, as I found out from this friend, my Mr European didn't like dating a woman who earned more than him. This little nugget of new information put a number of things into perspective for me. Our reunion coincided with me being promoted. I was clearly making more money than him. What should have been a happy occasion just added fuel to his already insecure fire and our relationship was short-lived. It didn't help that I had a brief liaison with another man. Yes, I was deeply hurt and disappointed, and somewhat guilty, but I'd get over it – I had a lot on my plate and my career was beckoning.

Fact: For the most part, there is a substantial pay gap between the genders. Women can be paid up to 17 per cent less than their male counterparts. However, research undertaken in the US has identified a type of 'earning reversal' phenomenon, which can occur in major cities. Data from the Census Bureau's American Community Survey was analysed by research company Reach Advisors. Of the 2,000 communities analysed, an overwhelming majority showed the average full-time salaries of young women as being 8 per cent higher than those of their male peers. Interestingly, this figure increases in major cities. For example, in New York it is 17 per cent! There is a caveat to this 'reverse gender pay gap', though: you need to be under thirty, single, childless and living in a city.

The conditions that are feeding this rise in female salaries include a growing knowledge-based economy with a declining manufacturing base, which are dominant trends in the US. It may take some years for this reversal to reach our shores. However, here in Ireland, we have a highly educated female population and an economy that is increasingly technology-led, as opposed to manufacturing-led, which make for favourable conditions for such a trend to manifest itself here.

It's hard to meet a decent guy in your thirties. There are a number of reasons for this: 1. A woman in her thirties is seen only to be interested in marriage and motherhood, as her biological clock is ticking. She sends out an odour (oblivious to her) that reeks of desperation and is highly toxic to any man who comes within an ass's roar of her; 2. A man is very challenged by a woman who, since she is in her thirties, has probably accumulated a certain amount of wealth and a sense of independence – traits that are alien to the Irish 'mammy's boy' syndrome; 3. Women in their thirties still believe that they will meet Mr Perfect with no baggage other than the mother-in-law from hell; 4. Men in their thirties are more likely to want to hook up with Barbie in her twenties; and, finally, 5. Your knight in shining armour is unlikely to seek you out as you opt for sloppys, slippers and a good soppy movie in instead of a night out on the tiles.

I wasn't always the stay-at-home type. For the past near decade I had become a workaholic as, one-by-one, my friends were lost to marital bliss, followed by the years of mayhem that is parenthood. Having a social life in your thirties is far different to in your twenties – especially if you're single. For starters, you have to plan a night out with friends weeks in advance as impromptu sessions have become a thing of the past. Your circle of friends also dwindles from the usual gang to a few diehards. You become the 'odd one out' overnight. As you ponder where it all went wrong, you begin to doubt yourself. If you get invited to dinner parties, it's usually to be set up with a geek – there just never seems to be enough eligible men to go around. You know what I mean. It's not as though you're overly fussy either. Personality has long since overtaken looks in your credentials column. Okay, hair most definitely is still a 'must have', but a beer belly is tolerable and poor style sense can be easily cured with a bit of retail therapy. Suddenly, before you know it, you're settling – you're looking at the geeks in a new light rather than being doomed to dust as a singleton.

Of course, there are bouts of bravery as you re-assure yourself that being single isn't all that bad, as you tuck into yet another tub of Ben & Jerry's. You're an independent lady with the look, loot and lots of 'L' factor (that's 'love' to you and me). You've a fantastic career and the freedom that married couples sometimes seem to envy. But these thoughts dissipate as the stark realisation of being left on the shelf soon begins to hit home – again. Perhaps it's a mid-life crisis, a decade too soon. I think I might have hit on a new phenomenon that has as yet to be diagnosed, dissected and debated. This is the singleton's man-a-pause.

For me, Mr Social (aka Mr Man-About-Town) was my saviour, albeit in the short term. He brought out the best and worst in me. I had known him for many years in a social context – but I didn't really 'know' him. I knew he fancied me. I wouldn't have been at all interested in him before, but, as I said, you look at potential partners in a different light as your clock ticks and your looks fade. We started dating and for six months it was bliss. To this day, I have no idea how I managed to maintain a healthy social life with little sleep in tandem with a hectic business schedule. The only night I stayed in was Monday night; weekends were spent sleeping until late afternoon. However, I was still averaging only about five hours sleep a night and I am most definitely a seven- to eight-hour woman. Soon things turned ugly as the cracks began to appear. These cracks coincided with the death of my mother, who had been ill for some months. We'd moved in together and initially it was a secure, loving environment where I readily admit I was the more vulnerable. Mr Social worked nightclub hours, whereas I worked office hours. I began to realise that, unless I pulled back on keeping up with his pace of life, my work and my health would suffer. I had already taken up smoking to the extreme. A destructive pattern was emerging. Alcohol and sleep deprivation took its toll. One argument too many, and it was all over between us within the year. While I nursed my wounds and went into recovery mode, he was already in another relationship and was married within a short time. When a guy tells you that he'll always love you, he probably does mean it – at the time! Lesson learned.

Did I tell you that I was suffering from a broken heart when my PA Julie decided to take action? Mr Social had really left a scar and, although it was a lucky escape, it hurt like hell. As a result, I had all but given up on motherhood but still craved a yang to my yin. I decided to take action and, for the year 2002, I set some clear personal rather than professional goals. Traditionally, I had always put work and more materialistic objectives as my top pursuits. Meeting Mr Right hovered around objective number five. But this year I decided to make Mr Right my number-one priority. I also decided to stop dating my ex-boyfriends. Some advice: if you want to move on, you need to stop going back. And, although there is merit in giving someone a second chance, any more than two is plain kidding yourself. This important lesson is probably one that you need to learn for yourself, but it can also apply to working relationships. I have a philosophy that if an employee wants to leave, let them go and don't take them back. Once they've uttered the words, the likelihood is that their ambitions are already elsewhere.

The best thing about broken hearts is that they not only mend, but they also prove that you haven't become a total cynic about life and love. That you have been hurt means you're still alive. Having cleared out all the cobwebs of past pursuits, I knew that I would need to meet someone totally new. I started getting myself in shape and putting myself out there. I went to every business and networking event for the first couple of months. After all, you just never know when Mr Right is going to turn up. I knew I was open to love again but, unfortunately, I only faced more and more disappointment as the months passed – all the single men were taken; I was too late! It slowly dawned on me that unless there was someone out there who had 'loved and lost' like I had, chances were I would have to seriously reassess my criteria for Mr Right. For starters, I had to probably accept that he was going to be separated or divorced. Otherwise I would be dealing with a confirmed bachelor or someone who was emotionally challenged. Isn't it strange how the word 'bachelor' conjures up images of men playing the field, whereas 'spinster' has more sinister, dejected undertones.

It was late March when Julie and I decided to take a more drastic approach to dating. In the absence of any real knights, we began to consider virtual possibilities. Internet dating was very new at the time and, indeed, quite taboo. Recently, a colleague had told me how he had been to a wedding where the couple had met 'through the Internet' as though it was some sort of alien encounter. I have to say I embraced this new dating method and was totally intrigued by the thousands of profiles on matchmaking websites supposedly looking for love. Reading through the profiles became my new hobby. It was a pleasant distraction from work and a somewhat sparse social calendar.

I decided to join up to an online dating agency, paid my membership fee and, within minutes, I began creating my profile. And, yes, I lied. I managed to knock at least five years off my age with the push of a button. I knew I looked younger, so how would anyone know? It would give me better odds and open up my dating parameters. I also described my weight as 'pretty normal' – I'm anything but normal in every sense of the word. In fact, I'd hate to be described as normal. It's a bit like being described as Ms Average, and who wants to be that?

It's quite therapeutic filling in your profile. Some questions are straightforward enough, like your star sign (as if that matters), personality, favourite cuisine and activities. But you do begin to wonder when you're asked what car you drive or what your favourite drink is. That said, doesn't a car tell you a lot about someone's personality? I decided not to put down the make of car I drove. Instead, I opted for a more cryptic answer: 'Fast car...I like to get there quickly.' Had I said a Merc convertible, I may have scared off half the possibilities and attracted perhaps some definite undesirables. Cars have always been an interest of mine. As a teenager, it was cool to date a boy with a car and, by the time you hit eighteen, the type of car seemed to really matter. It was a status symbol and it showed ambition and style. Of course, this criteria does change as you discover that fast cars usually mean fast guys. I've always loved cars. In fact, my Merc was probably my second most expensive purchase as a singleton. I had always aspired to own a particular model – the CLK convertible – and made it my business to reach that particular goal. On retrospect, it was outrageously expensive, totally unnecessary and very self-indulgent. But, to this day, I have never regretted that decision and I will probably never drive another car.

I described my ideal partner as: 'An eternal optimist, fun to be with, respectful and thoughtful. He should have a zest for life and love. Be balanced in personal and career life. Like fine wines, good company and not be afraid to show his affections'. I wasn't asking for much! I described myself as: 'Artistic, easygoing, humorous, outgoing, romantic, spontaneous and thoughtful'. I took these adjectives from the menu provided, but they seemed to fit the bill. When I pressed 'send', I was oblivious to the fact that that little action would change my life irrevocably.

It was easy to sift through the responses and, unfortunately, no one caught my eye. Joining an online agency is easy – taking the next step is a more daunting prospect. Inevitably, you write off each response with such judgements as: he must be married; he's too young, too old, too perfect, too smarmy. I looked at all the options, the risk and the possible reward. It soon became evident that those responding to my profile just didn't cut the mustard. Now, my mother always told me, 'Never run after a man or a bus as there will always be one behind.' But these were desperate times so I decided that, instead of waiting for Mr Maybe to contact me, that I might leave a message for him instead. I spent hours painstakingly looking through newly updated profiles. Those that were uploaded for more than a couple of weeks, I disregarded – there was obviously something wrong with them. Like a seasoned detective, I mulled over candidates, their personality traits and description. The exercise was more akin to finding a suitable employee than a soul mate! I finally managed to whittle my choice down to three and presented them to my PA for deliberation.

My first choice was an architect. He was bright, educated and appeared to be sensitive and a man of substance (a home owner). The more we communicated, the more creative I became. Before I knew it, we were lost in a fantastical world of poetry and prose. My communication was more akin to Brontë's *Wuthering Heights* and he matched me line-by-line. More importantly, his having been vetted by my PA, we decided to meet. Not one to put all my eggs in one basket, I also started to communicate with my number two choice, who incidentially didn't get the instant approval of my PA as he had some baggage.

Meeting a total stranger in a pub or club seems to be perfectly acceptable, as you are amongst friends in a social context. However, meeting someone who you've only communicated with through email is that bit more akin to a liaison dangereuse. Here I was meeting a guy who knew quite a bit about me, as I did about him. There was little doubt that there was chemistry there. But meeting him in the flesh could go three ways – it could go down like a lead balloon; develop into something more; or I'd be on the Nine O'Clock News, having been reported as a missing person. My biggest fear was of being found out – I had lied about my age and my figure was that bit more wholesome than I had described. I convinced myself that if that's all he was interested in then it wasn't meant to be. I took some safety precautions by way of telling my sister where I was going, whom I was meeting and at what time I would be back. I also decided to meet on a Saturday afternoon in a nearby pub. I arrived early and sat facing the door so that I would have a good view of people coming in. I waited patiently as lots of faces came and went. Eventually I got a text to say that he couldn't find me. This meant that he had passed me by, which wasn't a good sign. Of course, the converse was also true.

We eventually met and I spent the next two hours in deep disappointment, cringing. It was so obvious that I wasn't what he had expected. It didn't even matter what I thought of him as the body language was all wrong. Although I tried to lighten the mood, it was the longest blind date I'd ever been on and I wasn't keen to repeat the process any time soon. All communication ceased and I had learned a good lesson – don't let your imagination run away with you; it can only end up in disaster. But I guess that's the romantic in me. Once again, I threw myself into my work and put it down to a lesson learned. However, I was still communicating with 'Coldfeet', my number-two choice, as I didn't want to close off all possibilities immediately. He was far more down to earth than Number 1, with none of the Mills & Boon fantasy dialogue.

I liked his profile and how he described his ideal partner: 'A woman who is self-confident, intellectually challenging [note: not challenged intellectually!], out to work hard and achieve, and then play hard and relax. Friendship and honesty are everything in a relationship.' I felt I fitted the bill perfectly. He went on to include a quote by Tennyson: 'It is better to have loved and lost than to never have loved at all,' with the postscript, 'Anyone else out there looking to try again?' I guess it was the addendum that struck a chord with me. We began to communicate daily; it's amazing how honest you can be, if you feel the other person shares in this honesty. I remember in our early communications he asked if I had any baggage, to which I replied: 'With regard to the topic of baggage, the only type I like to carry is Louis Vuitton ... However, as I've never been able to afford such an expensive label, instead I have had to carry my last relationship for a lot longer than anticipated.' I went on to explain that, since my last relationship ended, I had managed to build a house, become managing director of a company, almost complete a Diploma in Applied Finance and buy the car of my dreams. Yes, girls, a broken heart can really focus the mind, so don't get mad, move on, multiply your portfolio, increase your dowry and canvass all your prospects! I also admitted to being 'high maintenance'. On the subject of five things I'd like to do that best describe me, I wrote:

1. On a sunny midweek day, abandon work and drive my convertible through the Wicklow mountains [note: I don't recall ever just taking off like this and would certainly only do so if I was accompanied by someone really special].
2. On a rainy day, be collected at work (preferably midday) and be whisked off somewhere romantic [note: again, wishful thinking].
3. On a weekend night, prepare dinner for my favourite company of friends [note: this was one of my more realistic social habits].
4. On a Friday night, have a quick drink after work and keep going into the wee hours, unplanned [note: definitely reminiscing here as this is something you do in your twenties and early thirties].
5. Take a bubble bath, listen to some great music and have a glass of really tasty red wine [note: this, believe it or not, still happens, although not as frequently as I'd like it to].

According to Coldfeet, 'We all carry baggage but it is those who deal with it who prosper.' He matched my five favourite things with:

1. A weekend on Achill Island or the West coast, no phone, etc....warm log fire, a fine bottle of port and good company [note: I gave this a high rating as it sounded perfectly idyllic].

2. An impulsive weekend away in New York, staying just off Times Square and enjoying good food in Little Italy and shopping for fakes in Chinatown [note: this hit all the boxes apart from buying the fakes – if you can't afford the real thing, save up or forget it].

3. A walk in Phoenix Park in mid-winter, followed by an afternoon session at Ryan's Bar [note: this was perfectly acceptable].

4. Seeing a damn good Premiership football match live, followed by a major night out in Liverpool [note: this was really a lad's night out and not one to be interfered with].

5. A night in with a major DVD – currently any De Niro/Pacino/Cage movie, a nice bottle of wine and a pair of slippers for my Cold Feet [note: ditto].

He had asked to meet me, but I declined the first time around as I really enjoyed our emailing and I didn't want to risk it ending. I was also in the middle of my exams and didn't need any unnecessary distractions. Four weeks passed and, in a sudden about turn, I agreed to meet. Now, Julie was monitoring developments carefully. As far as she was concerned, I was a great catch and should be very careful in making choices. Having given me the pep talk, and on realising that I was determined to give it a shot, she took a note of where and when we were going to meet and I got her guarded seal of approval .

We met on a sunny Thursday evening in June. I can even recall what I wore on the day. I didn't want to be overdressed and equally I didn't want to appear too casual. I wore a black top with a three-quarter-length red skirt and my sunglasses perched casually on my head, holding my hair back. I arrived on time and my stomach was in knots. We knew very little about each other physically, as it wasn't something that we actually went into previously. Would my lies get me into trouble again? As I walked through the lounge I got even more nervous. I scanned the whole room and it was on the second scout that I noticed someone reading a newspaper at the bar. As there were few single men around, I bravely approached in the hope that he was the right person.

He was. We sat down at seven and for almost five hours we talked and talked and talked. It was like meeting an old friend. If I was being really honest, I didn't like his suit and I didn't like his shoes. But I noticed that he had the most amazing blue eyes and fantastic English accent. I purposely drove so that I wouldn't drink much – there's nothing worse than having one too many and letting your guard down. I didn't fancy him but I really liked him. The bar was closing and he politely walked me to my car and pecked me on the cheek. There wasn't any awkward moment and I don't recall us making plans to meet again. I'm not sure if I wanted to meet him again. However, when I got home he had texted me to ask if I had arrived home safely. That one simple gesture really impressed me. We continued to communicate by email and met two more times.

It was after the third meeting that I confided to my sister that I wouldn't be meeting Coldfeet again. The reason was that he was really nice – too nice – and far too steady. Not one to mince words, she asked for his number as she thought it would be a good idea to tell him to act like an utter jerk as it would increase his odds with me. I realised that she was completely right. I had always gone for Mr Showoff, Mr Confident, Mr Self-Centred, and it had never worked out. I decided to meet Mr Steady one last time. It was the day after I'd finished my final exams and I remember being completely hungover. To this day, I'm not sure if it was the pressure of the exams which had dissipated or if my sister's words had resonated with me, but when Coldfeet walked through the door that day, I thought, 'Wow, he's really quite handsome.' The dress sense I could work on!

In addition, Mr Steady – David – was probably the first guy in a long time who had not only taken an interest in my work but was able to hold an informed discussion with me about it. In other words, he had brains to boot. That day was a defining one in my life as it was the day I made a decision to let this man into my world. Yes, he had baggage and lots of it. But it was his ability to work through his wounds and show a real strength of character; it was his amazing sense of devotion to his children and his sincerity that won me over. He had a total ease about himself, an inner calm and outward confidence that balanced so well with my more flighty personality. He was the yang to my yin and, in time, he was the man who would eventually win my heart and walk me down the aisle on what was to remain one of the happiest days of my life.

If I have any advice to impart, it is that the road to love is never smooth. Add to this a desire to have a good career, and sometimes your journey can lead you in many directions. It is only when you truly decide to put your personal goals ahead of your professional goals that you can expect to find love. They are not mutually exclusive, but both require your undivided attention and it's only when the time is right that everything will miraculously fall into place. We're all told that there are plenty of fish in the sea, that you have to kiss a lot of frogs before you find your prince – and, for the most part, this is true. However, you have to learn to be patient when fishing and to carefully choose those frogs before doing any kissing. And, although your heart might break on many occasions, it only takes 'the one' to mend it forever.

Chapter 5

Keep It Dynamic Stupid (KIDS)

'I don't think any woman needs to pretend to be superwoman but I think anything is possible.'

– Sarah Newman, serial entrepreneur, interviewed in WMB, issue 17

Month: May
Thought: Don't put off until tomorrow what you could do today!

I HAVE THREE PIECES of sound advice for women who want a career and children – don't leave it too late or leave it to luck; make sure you have the proper backup support in place; and accept that your life will change forever. Oh, and get a puppy first – it prepares you for that rocky road ahead!

Something happens at work when you become pregnant – you're treated differently. Of course, at first you think it's just the hormones, but as the bump gets bigger, your paranoia grows. You become overtly protective of your workspace, your projects and your career.

All too often, career women delay motherhood for so long that when the time is right for them, it may be too late. This, I'm sure, is one of the main reasons for our booming fertility industry. The average age for first-time mothers in Ireland is now thirty-one (my own mum was twenty) and giving birth over the age of forty no longer raises eyebrows (unless, of course, you're Cherie Blair). In Switzerland, 40 per cent of career women are childless. Is this out of choice? Is it a result of poor planning? Or is it evidence that a woman can't have it all? Decades of culture can also play its hand. In Germany, working women are still referred to as 'Rabenmütter' or 'raven mothers', after the black bird that pushes its chicks out of the nest. This is somewhat ironic, given that a woman, Angela Merkel, holds the highest post as Chancellor of Germany. She also ranks top of the Forbes 'World's 100 Most Powerful Women' list (2011), followed closely by US Secretary of State Hillary Clinton, President of Brazil Dilma Rousseff and Chief Executive of PepsiCo Indra Nooyi.

I have a theory that some ambitious women are attracted to a more maternal rather than material man – or perhaps they want both qualities. Of course, there's quite a difference between choosing a good father and choosing a stay-at-home husband. I believe that men should play a more pivotal role in a child's early years. There's much talk about paternity leave, but that's all it is. Ireland lags seriously behind in terms of the rights of fathers to paternity leave. One would think that common sense should prevail when dealing with the demands of a new baby. Are employers so out of touch that they cannot or will not recognise and anticipate the needs of a new parent at this important juncture? Yes, women have maternity leave but this legal right can still cause untold hardship for both the employer and expectant mother. From the day you tell your boss that you're expecting to the day you finally depart, both of you will experience a cornucopia of conundrums, not least the issue of who, if anyone, is going to cover your role while you're on leave.

In the UK, fathers are entitled to two weeks off work and receive a minimal payment from the state. In Norway, they receive up to ten weeks' paid leave. However, it is the Swedish model that has really taken paternity leave to another level. There, fathers receive two weeks' paid leave and an option of sharing sixteen extra months with their partner. Now, I'm not advocating any of these models for Ireland. I'm realistic about what the country can afford right now (which is zero), the extra burden that employers can take (again, zero) and the painfully slow manner in which our society and the law can evolve. However, if women are to operate in a more equal society, surely men need to be allowed embrace their parental roles, fully supported by society? I fear we have a long path to travel in this regard.

Some of Ireland's leading businesswomen comfortably admit that they have 'house husbands'. So, behind every successful woman is a man. This rare breed of man might be restricted to the elite top female earners. But perhaps house husbands are becoming more commonplace, as our distressed economy dictates which of the sexes loses their job first. In the EU, women have filled six million of the eight million new jobs created since 2000. In the US, three out of four people thrown out of work since the recession began are men (*The Economist* 2009). If this trend continues, women will become the breadwinners and men will have to don the aprons.

But there is still a vital few months when, physically and emotionally, mothers and their offspring need to bond. Even if fathers take up the reins, I would question at what stage this could or should happen. A friend of mine who runs a chain of florists admitted that she went back to work the day after giving birth. It was her busiest trading period and if she didn't, her business would have failed. Not many new mothers would have to make this difficult decision. We all remember the fallout in 2009 when

France's then Minister for Justice Rachida Dati returned to the Cabinet just five days after giving birth. Her actions created heated debate from many quarters. Dati perhaps added salt to some wounds with her sleek velvet attire and killer heels – she was more of a wonder woman than an ordinary woman. It does beg the question – how many women are in a position to take six months' leave and perhaps a further three months' unpaid leave without consequences for their career? Employers need to take a long-term view of their female workforce. The likelihood is that a female employee will be out of action at least twice, if not three times, within her career cycle. The bigger companies may be able to factor in paid maternity leave and experienced cover, but for most small employers it's a burden.

A lot can happen in six to nine months in a company's life. The expectant employee who leaves on maternity leave may return a very different individual – assuming she returns at all. Due consideration is needed by both sides – employer and employee – as to how individuals and companies can adjust to these changes. This has given rise to a new phenomenon called M-Coaching. Yes, Maternity Coaching is big business as employers and employees duck and dive their way through the matrix of emotions and demands. For many employers, it's a battle to retain their high-calibre women, as maternity leave frequently coincides with a critical point in women's careers, when they are on the partner or senior management track. If a woman takes advantage of the longer leave available, she decreases her chances of re-entering the workforce; many women opt out of their careers in favour of being full-time mums. Depending on a company's culture, other new mums choose part-time work or a less demanding career path in search of the perfect balance.

In more recent years, women are looking to the flexibility of consultancy work and even entrepreneurship. Redundancy has also driven women to consider these paths as they try to square their various commitments and balance household, child care and finances. I always encourage those who want to set up a business, but there is a caveat. Running your own business comes with a new set of rules. If you think you can look after your young children while maintaining a high level of professionalism, you'll end up in a tug of war. The only loser is you, as you stretch yourself too thin and begin to feel the guilt and strain of being neither a great mum nor a good businesswoman. If, as a mum, you choose the route of lifestyle entrepreneur, your expectations are very much geared toward family first and career/income second. Once you make this subtle choice, you can succeed within a more balanced framework and without losing your mind.

I joined the Nicole Kidmans, Helen Fieldings and Cherie Blairs of this world when I had my first and only child at forty. Of course, I was already a 'confidant' to my partner's two daughters – I don't like the word stepmum. The children already have a mum and, although 'we are all parenting', my role is that of loyal friend and hopefully role model. When I met David, his girls were only four and eight. The jump from thinking about me and 'us' to thinking about them was huge. At times, it was almost too hard to handle as the children were caught within the dynamics of a failed relationship with all the fallout that follows. But I grew to love them dearly. I have great respect for their ability to share themselves between two households without grumbling or complaining. I put much of this down to their father, who totally dotes on them and it is reciprocated tenfold.

David and I thought and talked many times about having a child. Our current lifestyle allowed us to enjoy alternate weekends to ourselves. It allowed us to maintain our demanding work schedules and it also somewhat addressed the 'kids' debate – at least for David, since he had already 'been there and done that'. However, there's something missing when your role is that of provider to children who are not your own. It's not akin to adoption and certainly isn't as difficult as fostering, I gather. But, still, I knew that there was a missing part to my parenting jigsaw.

A year into our relationship, I realised that I needed more. I wanted to have a baby – my commitment to and understanding of the idea of having children had already kicked in. To put it another way, my days of nightclubs and hangovers were already over and I was prepared to put away my dancing shoes for the foreseeable future. I saw a specialist to ensure my pipes were in perfect motoring order and, in January 2004, a year after deciding to 'go for it', I fell pregnant. (Isn't it ironic that you spend the earlier part of your life taking every precaution to avoid an unwanted pregnancy and the later part taking every action necessary to get pregnant?)

Unfortunately, I had a miscarriage within weeks of getting the blue line. Having a miscarriage can be traumatic for many and thousands of women go through this pain in silence. Although there are no official statistics for the number of miscarriages, it is estimated that up to one in four pregnancies end this way. I recall how sorry my doctor was at the time. I, on the other hand, looked on the positive side as it meant that I had the ability to conceive. I vividly recall having to be driven home by one of my work colleagues as I was haemorrhaging heavily. It was a long trip home that day as I held my secret loss deep inside. Two months later, I found out I was pregnant again and almost four months later I found the guts to tell my new shareholders.

At this stage, I had taken the leap from Mac Communications to the Neworld Group, who were a creative bunch of individuals involved in brand and web design. All they were missing was a publishing entity. In 2002, I launched Neworld Image and began the slow task of establishing a new publishing house from scratch. At least this time I had a vested interest. On reflection, Neworld was a small step on my journey to total autonomy. It was also a bit of a culture shock. I was used to delegating at Mac with an experienced team of more than thirty-five people around me. Now I was the team. I slowly began building up a publishing portfolio on the back of a decade or so of experience. There were challenges; probably the biggest was the manner in which the group operated. I was not privy to the operations of the other divisions but it became evident that if one division was struggling, it understandably put other divisions under pressure.

We gained some great publishing tenders and I continued to work hard and build a small, talented team around me. I also became more active in my industry networks and was nominated chairman of the Periodical Publishers Association of Ireland (PPA), the body representing Irish magazine interests. Networking is vital in any line of business. You need to invest your time in it and, although you receive no immediate monetary gain, you do make valuable contacts and build on your reputation and knowledge base. During this time, I also represented magazines on the Press Council Steering Committee.

At a time when I was engaged in building a new business and already wearing a number of hats, motherhood came knocking. There's never a 'right time' to have a baby. The build-up to telling my shareholders I was pregnant was stressful, and nothing was quite the same afterwards. I put much of this down to my own paranoia, but it was clear that everyone was surprised by the news and not all too happy. I guess I was only in the company a short time and so much was riding on my ability and availability to deliver the results. As the only female shareholder, my new condition challenged my co-shareholders who, although parents themselves, probably focused on the negative aspects – the prospect of sickness; the long maternity leave; the absence of an experienced leader in a relatively new venture; the possibility that I might not return.

Rebecca was conceived in an atmosphere that had 'positive'

stress rather than 'negative' stress – the latter can be harmful to a woman who wants to have a child. Such were the high levels of stress at my previous company, Mac, that it took a total change of atmosphere for this gift to be bestowed. I would advise any woman who wants to conceive to look at her working environment to see what stresses are present. I'm not advocating a mass exodus strategy, just be cognisant of any pressures around you and evaluate your position. Some people thrive on stress and I certainly have been known to rise to the occasion. But if having a baby is your number one goal, don't be surprised if stress is part of the reason why it's taking that bit longer to conceive. Although this view has been based largely on anecdotal or indirect evidence (and indeed my own experience), a study by researchers at Oxford University and the US National Institutes of Health suggests that high stress levels may indeed delay your chances of becoming pregnant.

I was more determined than ever to remain focused. I had launched a publishing house under the Neworld umbrella and we were in our infancy. It was vital that I planned the next months carefully. I always arrived early to work and put in 100 per cent. In fact, my new condition suited me down to the ground and I relished every moment. They do say you glow when pregnant but they never mention the fantastic attention you get. You feel really special both inside and out. However, one of the not-so-helpful side effects, at least for this career girl, was the 'pregnancy brain' or 'baby brain drain', as it is sometimes referred to. This can occur during the first and third trimesters. Symptoms include short-term memory loss and forgetfulness. Although some doctors believe it's a myth, I'd hazard a guess that these are the male of the species. My desk was an array of pink post-its and I continuously wore my ring on a different finger to remind me that I had to remember something – more often than not, I just couldn't recall what that all-important something was. There were times when I was absolutely exhausted and as the pregnancy progressed I had a love affair with my bed and my couch – in fact, with anything remotely horizontal. I was due on 10 December and I remember thinking that I probably shouldn't go out for the few weeks before my due date just in case my waters broke. However, my attitude changed with time as I became less self-conscious. Perhaps it was all the prodding and monitoring I had to endure.

I purchased only two books during and after the birth and found myself jumping between *Your Baby and Child* by Penelope Leach and Rob Parson's *The Sixty Minute Mother*. According to child-care guru Leach: 'Any extension of choice is a cause for celebration…it can take time to adjust if you have been working for twenty years, but older women have more experience of life to bring to being parents' (quoted in Jardine 2010). Having to 'adjust' was putting it mildly, Penelope!

I worked up to and including my due date. My shareholders had taken the unusual step of bringing in a 'consultant' to work through the business plan for the coming year(s), which did put an additional strain on me and certainly on my patience – anyone would have thought that I wasn't coming back. On reflection, they were only protecting their investment but probably went about it in the wrong way. Of course, publishing was and is my passion and I had already made up my mind that I would return sooner rather than later. Research tells us that about a third of women want to stay home with their children, a third of them want a career and a third want both. I sat firmly in the final camp. Rebecca was born ten days after her due date and my only fear was that I'd have to spend Christmas in what I referred to as the 'Hotel'. Yes, Mount Carmel Hospital had a reputation for being pricey (I had private health cover), but it was perfect if you wanted some one-on-one attention. The midwives were amazing and they provided a valuable resource for a first-time mother. The most common word I used during the birth was 'epidural'. I won't recount the actual birth, but suffice to say that from the moment you hold your baby in your arms you'd do it all over again.

Rebecca was born at 1.10 p.m. on a Monday afternoon and weighed 8lbs 2ozs. And, yes, she was indeed 'fair of face'. She was the most perfect little baby that I'd ever seen. When you're an older mother, you worry about having a not-so-perfect child. That sounds so shallow, but it's true. Building up to the big day, you become even more anxious. I thanked God that day for Rebecca, who remains the most perfect miracle that I've ever experienced.

Staying at home was never on the cards. I have this theory that if you take away the 'something' that you're passionate about in life (in my case it was publishing) a part of you will die inside. I always knew that I would grow to regret the decision to leave my career if I'd taken that particular route. I wanted my daughter to be proud of me and to learn to value my work ethic. I also knew that I would appreciate the time I had with her as a working mum. Fortunately the solution to my child-care needs was close at hand. My sister Marion was a godsend. A stay-at-home mum herself, Marion had agreed to look after Rebecca part time when I returned to work, at least for the first year. This gave me a huge sense of security as my only other options would have been an au pair or a full-time nanny. I do wonder how other women cope. Many of my friends opted out of their careers in favour of full-time motherhood. But I think this was preordained. I envied the fact that they had their parents close by who could take up the slack when they needed a break. But not all of us are that lucky. I have huge admiration for the thousands of women who play the role of mother, wife, sister, daughter, carer and career girl. I know many women in management and owner/managers who have two, three and four children and seem to maintain a sense of balance in their personal and professional lives. Would men be able to cope with such responsibility?

In my mother's day, although men were the breadwinners

there was always a strong woman behind them, propping them up – looking after the household matters and caring for the needs of their young. Yes, men were the breadwinners but women were and remain the nurturers. A lot has changed down the decades and now, in 21st century Ireland, women mix the roles of motherhood and role model as they forge forwards in their careers of choice. But nothing can prepare you for motherhood. In the days up to Rebecca's birth, I was working to deadlines. In the weeks following her birth, I couldn't even find the time to make myself a cup of tea. I still can't understand how one tiny creature can play such havoc with your schedule. I cried profusely when David returned to work, having taken a week's holidays. He has always been such a confident dad and I just didn't know how I was going to cope without him. But paternity leave wasn't an option. I put my distress down to baby blues, as I muddled my way through changing nappies, baby baths and feeding.

My first expedition with Rebecca was a disaster. For starters, I refused point blank to get rid of my two-door sports car. I had the attitude of 'Have baby; will travel' and that nothing needed to change. So, here I was in my two-door soft top, wondering how on earth I was going to get baby and buggy on board. The car was so impractical and my back constantly ached as a result of stretching into the back seat to lift the baby complete with baby car seat in and out. Of course, I was totally in denial. I wasn't prepared to give up that little part of me that still wanted to fly solo. But that's exactly what happens when you become a mum. You realise over time that this baby needs everything that you have to give and more. It begins to dawn on you that, by gaining a beautiful addition to your life, you need to make more space. You sacrifice a bit more of yourself day by day, until you wake up one morning and think, 'Where has "me" gone?' Yes, there is a sense of 'identity loss' as motherhood develops and it takes quite a while to get your mojo back. There are no real instructions for motherhood. Even a basic thing such as buggy assembly and collapse can be a challenge. On my first outing, it took an hour and a half and a lot of sweat and tears to complete that daunting task of getting the buggy into the compact car boot.

I took six weeks' maternity leave before I returned to work, albeit on a part-time basis initially. It was a far cry from the standard six months allowed. I didn't want to get used to being at home and I knew that I had a huge task ahead of me to get the publishing venture up to speed. I never did get the knack of the breast pump and opted for bottles within months. You soon realise that you do have to be Superwoman to balance all the balls that are in your space. I found it difficult to divide my day – businesswoman until 2.00 p.m. and then the mad dash home to be a mother for the remainder of the day. The missed lunches and sleep deprivation, on top of publishing deadlines, soon took their toll. I was fortunate in many ways to be able to return to work quickly so that I could manage motherhood and career in my own flexible way. As a director, I had to deliver but it didn't matter how. Of course, as an employer I had to always be professional and lead by example. I knew my limitations and, within months of giving birth, I had revised my work routine several times until it worked for everyone.

Once Rebecca turned one, she started going to our local crèche part time and my sister continued to care for her while I worked. The crèche accommodates the working parent. Unlike our educational model, this system is not flawed. You can drop your child early and manage to get to work at a reasonable hour. You don't have to prepare lunch, as it's provided, and you can pick up your child at a realistic hour in the evening. It's also comforting to know that there are plenty of other parents in the same boat. There are always birthday parties to attend and a good sense of camaraderie between parents. At a crèche, your child gains social skills early.

I learned to work through any guilty feelings almost immediately. I didn't really have the 'tug of war' emotions that other parents seemed to have. I believe if you've thought through the options carefully and made an informed decision, it's best to get on with it. A good crèche is a godsend to a working parent but it can become cost prohibitive if you have more than one child to accommodate. It's not unusual to see women cope with child and career after their first but bow out of full-time work on the second or third. I don't know what the solution to this is. I had thought that greater tax relief for working parents might be an option as it would encourage women to remain in the workforce. But perhaps this would just drive up crèche fees even further. At the end of the day, unless there is a concerted drive to create more family-friendly policies at government level and corporate level, not much can change. Women will continue to question the viability of staying at work once the costs of child care are calculated. This issue is the single biggest challenge facing a woman who wishes to maintain a career she's passionate about and be a loving mother. Some refer to these women as 'wanting to have it all'. I believe we just want to have a choice.

For me, mixing motherhood and management is a continuous learning curve, right down to which school to choose for my daughter. I recall when I was first pregnant that it was vital to put your name on the school registrar to be guaranteed a place. Needless to say, I found this suggestion totally absurd – I had plenty of more pressing issues front of mind. As Rebecca approached four, the Celtic tiger had stopped roaring and the school waiting lists, as a result, had diminished. I was fortunate to have my daughter enrolled in our local private school, which had been totally renovated the year previously. This marked the start of a new reality for this working mum.

The school gates opened at 8.30 a.m. and closed promptly for K1 (Kindergarten to you and me) at 12.30 p.m. After-school facilities were almost non-existent, not to mention cost prohibitive. I had just gotten used to crèche hours and was now presented with a whole new set of rules and challenges. My sister came to the rescue (once again) and we planned itineraries to meet our various lifestyles.

Rebecca didn't take to her new surroundings too readily. She was boisterous by nature, which was a prerequisite when playing with the boys at her crèche. However, she was now attending an all-girls school where a certain level of decorum was expected. I'm not quite sure why I picked an all-girls school. I guess it was because I had attended one. Its proximity to home was a deciding factor, as was the fact that my sister's children also attended. There were some interesting school policies. For instance, if you had a party, everyone in the class had to be invited. I do agree with the principle of this as no one feels left out. Also a party for twenty girls can go off much smoother than one with both boys and girls. Rebecca, sporting her beautiful blue and white smock with hair neatly tied back (sometimes), became accustomed to changing from outdoor to indoor shoes according to the rules. But she was still wayward and was the cause of many hours of anxious debate.

Rebecca is now in P1 (First Class) and mother and daughter are doing well. She has adapted well to her new surroundings; she has learned to understand the difference between a group hug and a group tug, for instance. I do feel in the minority – probably because I am in the minority – as a working mum among the parents of the children in her class. There are the cliques that you have no hope of ever infiltrating. These parents are not unwelcoming. They work hard to keep house and home in order. They always volunteer for school drop-offs, fundraising events and school games. They play an intricate part in keeping extracurricular activities going. For this I am extremely grateful. But they operate in a very different environment with different expectations, ambitions and needs to me. Perhaps this is the invisible shield that separates us: we are inherently different with one common bond – our daughters.

Getting the work–life balance right takes years of practice and constantly takes you outside your comfort zone. I view it as a work-in-progress, which will need constant realigning. As the needs of those around me change, I will need to anticipate them to ensure that I can offer the right amount of support and guidance, while maintaining my identity. All the while, I continue to operate outside my comfort zone. There is much debate around parenting and I have, as yet, to finish reading John Gray's *Children Are from Heaven: Positive Parenting Skills for Raising Cooperative, Confident and Compassionate Children* (yes, the same author who wrote *Men Are From Mars, Women Are From Venus*). According to Gray, 'We're at a crisis point in history. All of the old parenting skills we learned by watching our parents parent are not as effective as they used to be. Children today are different, and do not respond to guilt trips, yelling, and the threat of punishment' (interview available on www.medicinenet.com). So, as I speed read through his pages in the hope of becoming a better parent, I recognise that I have three girls under my wings – all at different phases of their young lives, each with unique qualities, each with individual needs. Two may not be my own flesh and blood, but I provide for them and nurture them as if they were my own. One is working towards her final years in school, another is only starting out in her senior years and the third is, of course, only finding her feet. Will I embark on Gray's 'confident and compassionate' journey for the answers or will I opt for the more hard-hearted approach employed by our Chinese counterparts? *Battle Hymn of the Tiger Mother* by Yale Law School professional Amy Chua is a how-to guide for Western parents who want to learn the methods Chinese parents use to raise, as Chua puts it, 'so many maths whizzes and music prodigies'. I don't think so!

I have never regretted the path I've chosen. Yes, I have been tested with tears and no doubt will be tested again, often. Plato offers some sound words, though: 'Do not train a child to learn by force or harshness; but direct them to it by what amuses their minds, so that you may be better able to discover with accuracy the peculiar bent of the genius of each.' It is this same genius that will guarantee a child's future happiness.

Chapter 6

Failure Is Not an Option

'You need a unique idea, you need to be passionate, and you have to be willing to work hard. And most important, you need to trust your gut.'

– Bobbi Brown, make-up artist and founder of Bobbi Brown Cosmetics; interviewed in *WMB*, issue 21

Month: June
Thought: If you dream it, you can do it.

WHILE REBECCA was growing into a little person, I was becoming more aware of the reality of my working environment and less enamoured with it. I still felt a bit of an outsider, which was probably down to the fact that I was the 'last one in'. However, I worked hard and remained very passionate about publishing. The contract side of the business was developing at a steady pace and we had secured some great tenders. However, I also knew that contracts would come and go and 'owning' a title was where it was all at.

It was as far back as the early noughties when I first had the concept of a business magazine for women floating around in my head. Newspapers had a male majority readership and the existing business titles offered little for the female reader. The glossy women's magazines were great if you were interested in fashion or food, but there was definitely a gap in the market for a magazine that targeted the career-minded woman. However, it wasn't until 2006 when I started developing the concept for such a magazine to the point where I had a template of how it should look, its editorial ethos and a clear marketing strategy. I showed my plans to launch *WMB – The Irish Magazine for Businesswomen* to my shareholders, who were a bit taken aback at how far I had developed the concept. It was made clear that, unless it was a self-financing initiative, there would be no investment. This was a bit of a shock but I remained undeterred, as I knew deep inside that this was what I'd always wanted to do. I developed a great keynote presentation and started touting to the ad agencies with mixed success.

Selling an existing product or service is a challenge in itself. Selling a vision is nearly impossible. At one point I remember sitting opposite a well-groomed, suited agency woman, her blonde hair cascading across her straightened shoulders.

'Rosemary,' she said, 'I just don't see it. Where are you going to get all the material for your magazine?' Her inference was clear. I thought, 'If this woman can't get the concept for *WMB*, I'm screwed.' I told her that I was inundated with features and possibilities. I rhymed off international brands such as Ann Summers, Coffee Republic and Bobbi Brown; I listed those women on our very own doorstep – Danuta Gray, Tanya Airey, Mairead Sorensen. One thing I wouldn't run out of, I told her, were female role models. I said that the beauty of *WMB* – our unique selling point – was that it had never been done before. There were fashion magazines for women but there was nothing out there that would satisfy the savvy woman.

'It's about connecting women, offering them a new platform to reflect, collaborate, connect and gain knowledge from one another,' I said. 'If you pick up any of the current Irish business and lifestyle titles, you'd be hard pressed to find one that satisfies today's businesswoman – one that is aimed specifically at her, one which addresses her individual needs and one that talks her language.'

As I walked away from the meeting, saddened by the connotations our conversation had thrown up, I too felt like throwing up! This woman was meant to be 'one of us', an intelligent, hardworking, supportive multitasker. However, she was a non-believer and I couldn't assimilate her. She didn't think there were enough successful businesswomen and female entrepreneurs to fill the pages of a magazine on a regular basis. I knew I had a battle on my hands and it wasn't from the opposite sex.

I struggled to reach my first advertising target on *WMB*, but then I was publisher, editor, writer, production manager and sales executive all rolled into one. *WMB* was also just one of my projects on the go and I was a young mother to boot. I've always said that the title MD should stand for 'Mad Dog' as you need to be nuts to want it. In between other projects, I was pulling together a vision with a tiny team and no budget to speak of. If I had stopped to think for one moment, *WMB* would never have happened. A more realistic approach would have been to bring together a dedicated sales team, a host of writers, a sub-editor, a creative team, merchandising personnel and that all-important investor with deep pockets. But thinking about the 'how' can dampen one's ardour. In my experience, the trick is to just do it.

The front cover of issue 1 was simply inspirational. It was a shot of a woman holding her hand up to a shattered window. The format of the magazine was what is referred to as 'bastard' size – too wide to be a typical magazine size – which hopefully would allow it to stand out on the retail shelves. It was different in every aspect, right down to its spinal message. It also displayed the four core editorial values on each spread: Aspiring, Individual, Visionary and Passionate. The aim was (and continues to be) for each feature to emulate these values. I went about searching for great writers who would be equally as fervent. It was time consuming and sometimes difficult to balance their fees against my non-existent budget. I remember meeting one well-known contributor and feeling somewhat intimidated at first. She agreed to be a contributor on the single condition that I would pay her within thirty days of invoicing. If I didn't, she wouldn't write for me again. I thought, 'Well that's one straight-talking lady.' She still writes for *WMB* to this day.

Many people wonder how I came up with the name for the magazine. I knew that the Web would be a very important part of my business model down the line, so I wanted a title that could be easily tagged, something that would pop up if you entered 'women' and 'business' in a search engine. Names went around the houses and, after much brainstorming, I came up with *Women Mean Business*. It gets a mixed reaction, but the important thing is that it gets a reaction. There's nothing worse than having an identity that everyone forgets. It's a bit of an oxymoron, as your 'identity', your brand, should be individual and unique. So, while I was at risk of offending some people, I wanted to hopefully appeal to more. I immediately bought the domain name and I recall that, within a week of purchasing it, someone offered to buy it, which I took to be a great omen at the time. *Women Mean Business* wasn't going to be just a magazine; it was a brand that would organically grow.

I always appreciated the importance of intellectual property. If you think about it for a moment, you'll realise that publishing is all about intangibles. So you need to protect your creative. I was fortunate to have worked with one of the best intellectual property solicitors in Ireland, who also happened to be a woman. In fact, she has contributed to *WMB* since its inception and is as passionate about all things legal as I am about all things publishing. We started the process of trademarking the brand and quickly realised that *Women Mean Business* was too generic. Eventually, we settled on *WMB – the Irish Magazine for Businesswomen*, while our website womenmeanbusiness.com would form an integral part of the *WMB* brand. It was a great learning curve and, if you search for our website under *WMB* magazine or *Women Mean Business*, we're always in the top results found.

Our main interview in issue 1 was with Danuta Gray, CEO of O2 Ireland at the time. In it she admits: 'I made a very conscious decision that I wanted to get as far as I could by the time I was 35, and only then would I consider having children. My choice was to go as far as I could early.' This strong and determined woman seems to have carefully mapped out her path and fortunately she got all that she desired. Another role model to participate in our launch edition was the then managing director of Grafton Recruitment Aine Maria Mizzoni, who has a theory about women and glass ceilings. 'They are easy to shatter,' she says, 'Once you realise they don't exist.' She admits she encountered a few barriers along the way in her career, but believes that the only ceilings women can't break through are 'the ones we create ourselves'. Both interviews are still very relevant five years on as women continue to be challenged by juggling motherhood with the mighty demands of management. For me at the time, though, I soon faced a challenge that would stretch me way beyond my comfort zone. We'd planned our launch edition of *WMB* for the end of February 2006. I opted not to have a traditional 'big bash' as I'd no budget and, more importantly, I believed that a launch party was somewhat premature and I preferred to wait until I had something to celebrate. There were three weeks to go to print when disaster struck.

It was a damp Tuesday, like most other evenings in February. I had made the mad dash to collect my toddler, get home and put the dinner on for everyone. David arrived in with the two girls and, within minutes, he began trembling incessantly. He practically collapsed on the coach in front of us all. I immediately rang my sister (who was a qualified nurse) and then I rang for an ambulance as my gut told me something was terribly wrong. Fifteen minutes later, I'd left the children in the care of my sister and I was on the way to the hospital with David, who was a shivering wreck. They brought him straight through A&E and, within hours, he had undergone a lumber puncture with suspected meningitis. The doctors couldn't get his temperature down and I was allowed stay with him as they monitored him closely. These were the longest and hardest hours of my life as I stood over him totally helpless. No one was able to tell me what was wrong because nobody knew. Everyone was waiting for his temperature to subside, but it didn't. In all, he was subjected to three lumber punctures and all manner of examinations. It transpired that he had contracted septicemia and any delay in getting help would have been fatal. As he lay there totally incapacitated I felt so vulnerable. I would have swapped places with him in a heartbeat. I found out later that septicemia (or blood poisoning) is a serious, life-threatening infection that gets worse very quickly. It can begin with spiking fevers, chills, rapid breathing and rapid heart rate. The death rate is high – more than 50 per cent.

The following days were crucial and he received the best of care. He remained in hospital for two weeks as they prodded and poked, examined and diagnosed. He was tested from head to toe and his blood cultures were regularly analysed. It transpired that an angiogram he had undergone some twenty-four hours before falling ill was likely to have been the cause of his blood poisoning. It was highly possible that the catheter, which was placed into the blood vessel in his groin, was infected. Probably most people would have hit the roof at hearing this, but we were just so relieved to find out what was wrong with him. We put it down as an experience better forgiven but not necessarily forgotten. I was so happy to have him back home again and safe. I knew that I could have lost him. It hadn't escaped me that I was around the same age as my mother when she was widowed. Nothing can prepare you for such a scare and you are left asking yourself the question, 'What if?'

The first issue of *WMB* eventually went to print a couple of months later than planned in May 2006. The only people who really noticed its delay were the small crew of passionate individuals who had put their hearts and souls into its creation. Thereafter, it would be produced on a bi-monthly basis and to deadline! I loved everything about *WMB* and wanted to really spend time developing the brand. However, that would cost money and unfortunately there wasn't the desire among my shareholders to invest hard cash into the project at the time. My gut told me that this was an opportunity not to be missed. It was time to part ways and build my own business – on my own.

It was a difficult exit for all concerned but what breakup isn't? I bought out any interest in the *WMB* brand. However, to this day, I still work on projects with Neworld as they're a great bunch of talented individuals. On retrospect, I was fortunate to have crossed paths with them, as the jump between Mac Communications and setting up my own business might have been too much of a culture shock for this gal's system.

Setting up totally solo was scary to say the least. I was brimful of ideas, but had only a team of two behind me: a good right-hand girl who had recently graduated and was keen to learn and a very gifted designer who really got what I was trying to achieve. I needed finance and, from the outset, I knew my take-home pay was going to take a hell of a nose dive. These are the sacrifices that you make when you set up your own business. Money as a major motivation is replaced by a desire to realise your vision. Of course, I still had a mortgage to pay, food to put on the table and other considerations. I had David's full support and we made a five-year commitment to the project. This was the 'security blanket' that I needed to proceed. I set up a limited company and ensured all the legalities and accounting procedures were in place.

After this, the next step was to meet with the bank. I had prepared realistic three-year projections, had a great track record and was experienced. I also had a good relationship with my local bank, which was built up over a number of years. However, publishing by its nature is hard to understand if you're not directly involved in it. In its infancy, it's about building a brand which one day will have real value. But explaining this to a young pimple-faced loan advisor who seemed to be just out of school shorts proved more difficult than anticipated. I only managed to secure an overdraft and even that had to be personally guaranteed. I opted to remortgage the house instead, which incidentally was with another bank. Fortunately, it was at a time when there was cheap money, tracker mortgages and few questions asked. The house was also a very valuable asset, so I was taking a calculated monetary risk. At worst, I would have to sell up and clear any debts with some money to spare; at best, I would be successful and could pay the loan back.

There is a belief that women are risk averse and that, in fact, women themselves either believe this to be the case or they are unaware of the risks they take during their 'normal' working lives. In a financial context, I would argue that women usually only borrow what they feel they can afford to repay. Women play it somewhat safe and build their businesses more organically, more slowly. The adage 'The bigger the risk, the greater the reward' comes to mind. Perhaps this is why we're not attracted to or attractive for the venture capitalists who like high returns more quickly.

Unlike our male counterparts, we tend to calculate financial risk. Our approach of putting reason rather than recklessness behind decisions could have saved current and future generations much financial pain. Indeed, in Iceland women booted the alpha males out of power for causing its shattering economic crisis that broke in 2008. In 2009, Johanna Sigurdardottir was elected prime minister and vowed to bring an end to Iceland's 'age of testosterone'. Iceland took over from Norway as the country with the smallest gender gap. According to the 2009 World Economic Forum Report, Iceland achieved this ranking with high scores in education, political empowerment and economic participation.

If women have been painted as risk averse, it may be an undeserved label. The same year Iceland voted in a female prime minister to sort out the country's economic woes, the Simmons School of Management (SOM) in Boston collaborated with brand giant Hewlett-Packard to explore women's risk-taking behaviour. Their findings were included in their report: *Risky Business: Busting the Myth of Women as Risk Averse.* Over 650 managerial women responded to questions about risks they had taken, the factors that influenced their decisions and the outcomes of those decisions. According to the findings: 'Women do indeed take risks: a vast majority of women in their survey embraced professional opportunities that involved high-risk probabilities.'

However, despite strong support in the survey findings for the theory that women embrace risk, and that an overwhelming majority embrace activities involving what the press might consider 'cowboy' levels of high risk, in the business world women are still viewed as risk averse. According to the authors of the report, there may be two reasons for this: 'First women's actual risk-taking may be invisible and so goes unrecognised; second, women may be enacting role-congruent behaviours that are interpreted, through a male lens, to be risk averse.' An example of the latter is when women tap into their professional networks and seek advice. This may be seen as being indecisive.

Ironically, female role-congruent behaviours, such as inclusive decision making and collaboration, are cited as some of the reasons women are often asked to take on the high-risk situations of turning around organisational or country crises.... The challenge for women might not be how to take risks, as they already do so. Instead, it may be making those risks visible and capturing the credit for risk-taking in ways that signal their success to those around them. (Simmons School of Management 2009)

Armed with the new knowledge that women take risks and happy to join this new network of growing deviants, I launched WMB Publishing on a wing and a prayer, initially operating out of my aunt's house in the city centre. We had one phone line that we fought over constantly and an intermittent network service, which isn't great when you need to send a magazine to print. We worked away under the radar for a couple of months. I was also planning my wedding in the little spare time that I had left. Two weeks before David and I were due to be married, I got a quite official looking letter questioning the 'use' of the premises as it was a residential area. I knew there were many people working from their homes on the street but I guess someone didn't like the idea of us being there. But for every door that closes, another one opens. Within a couple of hours of receiving the nasty warning, I found offices for rent literally around the corner from us on Harrington Street. Over the following weekend we moved (again) and two weeks later I was on my honeymoon.

Looking back on this, I'm not too sure how I kept everything together. But it does help when you work with individuals who are almost as passionate and as positive about the business as you.

Life Lesson: Surround yourself with positive people and don't allow negative speak into your personal and professional space.

An example of making positivity work for you is to not use the word 'try'. If you try to do something or try to go somewhere, it seldom happens. However, if you replace 'try' with 'do', you'll quickly find that you're far more productive.

There were four aspects to my business model – the flagship title *WMB* magazine; a website which initially was to be a reflection of the magazine with plans for a portal site; contract publishing which was limited to high-end clients only; and, finally, conferencing and awards. I only wanted to employ four people within WMB and all other services would be outsourced. This suited my overheads, the space we were operating in and the appetite out there for flexible working arrangements. I had learned from the previous businesses I worked for that when you employ a lot of people, you suddenly become a human resources expert and your main passion takes second place. My team of four consisted of a creative designer, a passionate editorial and research assistant (aka my right-hand woman), an energetic sales head and me. I was fortunate in securing two of my key players and for the most part I kept the dual roles of managing editor and sales head! From time to time I had someone helping me with sales. I slowly grew advertising in the magazine and we were never short of copy to include. Over the following months, we were stretched as we put great issues to bed with tight resources. We interviewed fantastic women who were both established and only setting out in business – Mary Davis, director of the Special Olympics; France Ruane, director of the ESRI; an exclusive with Assistant Garda Commissioner Catherine Clancy; and an explosive piece with Patricia Lewis, the then director of UNIDIR (United Nations Institute for Disarmament Research), who also happens to be a nuclear physicist and specialist on arms.

Of course, when you're building a title and a company, the money only goes one way – out! I recall having lunch with a group of ladies to celebrate a friend's birthday and I sat beside

Maeve Donovan who was Managing Director of the *Irish Times* at the time. We swapped pleasantries and she asked about WMB. I indicated that it was going well and that I hoped to break even within three years. Maeve, with a knowing smile, gently placed her hand on my shoulder and whispered, 'You may want to give yourself five, Rosemary.' Her intentions were good, but I remained more determined than ever to prove her wrong. The result? Well, let's just say we had an unprecedented intervening couple of years brought on by the 'Great Recession'! In order to keep the company liquid, we undertook contract publishing work. It was a hard slog but when you're enthusiastic and you're working towards a goal, your energy levels soar.

I had a huge desire to arrange an event that would get women networking and, to this end, I decided to host the inaugural WMB Conference & Awards in 2007. I could clearly visualise what I wanted to achieve and, although I didn't quite know how I was going to get there, I just went for it. I set about finding a unique speaker for the day. To secure a speaker, you can work through an agent or you can go directly to him or her and then be referred to their agent. The bottom line is to negotiate the fee. As I wanted to bring in female speakers from abroad who hadn't been exposed in Ireland previously, it was a more difficult task. I not only had to find the right motivating and successful individual, but I then had to convince him or her to travel to Ireland for an event that had never taken place before.

My first keynote speaker was Jacqueline Gold, managing director of the highly successful Ann Summers chain. Reputed to be one of the richest women in England, this reserved, petite brunette was passionate and personable. She openly admitted: 'Ann Summers would not be the success it is today if I was not a woman.' Gold recounted the story of how she was posted a letter with a bullet in it when she first opened her store in Dublin's O'Connell Street. I guess her business and her accent didn't quite fit in on Dublin's main street at the time. In addition, I managed to convince the motivational guru Jack Black to speak. I knew that if the audience got a fraction of his MindStore message, they would be inspired to lead a more balanced and positive life.

Of course, I couldn't put the show on without sponsors and, with much negotiation, I managed to secure O2 as our title sponsor. At the time, O2 was run by Danuta Gray (who, as mentioned, featured in our first issue of *WMB*) and she also agreed to speak on the day. A number of blue chip clients sponsored each of five awards.

I can't relate how difficult it was to balance all the balls and at times I really thought I had bitten off more than I could chew. However, I really believed in what I wanted to achieve for this event and, five years on, I still put myself through the mill to ensure it attracts the media interest it deserves, inspires women to engage and continues to recognise all that is wonderful in the world of women.

Chapter 7

All Red but Where's the Black?
Cash Flows and more Cash Flows

'Women are assets. Women are agents of change and assets. An economy that does not recognise its assets is doomed to suffer.'

— Irene Khan, former Amnesty International secretary general; interviewed in
WMB, issue 21

Month: July
Thought: Learn something new.

I WOULD NEVER WISH to be colour blind, but sometimes it would be good to see a bit more black and a lot less red when I review my cash flows. Gypsy Rose Lee was one of my fancy dress characters way back when you didn't have to take yourself too seriously. I could read your fortune and see into the future, painting a convincing picture – all in the name of fun and a few glasses of red wine. But no one tells you that you need to be a clairvoyant to project, plan and produce the profit lines for a business. You also need to have Lady Luck on your side.

Eamon de Valera

Dad and President de Valera – I now know where my smile came from!

Our very first issue of *WMB* launched in April 2006 – let the journey begin!

Jacqueline Gold, Ann Summers; Danuta Gray, O2 Ireland; Hilary O'Meara, Accenture; Rosemary Delaney, WMB; Kristina Grimes, Apprentice runner-up; Jack Black, MindStore at my first WMB Conference in 2007.

THE IRISH MAGAZINE FOR BUSINESSWOMEN

WMB
WOMENMEANBUSINESS.COM

Image is Everything

Communication is Key

Also in this issue »
OCTOBER | NOVEMBER 2008
€4.95 | £3.45 | ISSUE 16

VAL QUINN
MD, Coca Cola Ireland

V.I.BUSINESSWOMAN
Julia Ross, Ross Human Directions

O2 WMB CONFERENCE & AWARDS
'The Results Are Out!'

TINA ROCHE
CEO, BITC Ireland

COPING WITH UNCERTAINTY
Mindstore's Jack Black Advises

THE BUSINESS OF BRANDING
Adverse Advertising

October–November 2008 issue of
WMB.

Me and Karren Brady, TV personality and vice-chairman of West Ham United Football Club. What a fantastic role model! WMB Conference 2008.

May 2009 issue of *WMB*.

Adventurer Pat Falvey in an animated pose at the WMB Conference in 2008.

THE IRISH MAGAZINE FOR BUSINESSWOMEN

WMB

WOMENMEANBUSINESS.COM

The Business Of Beauty

From The Inside Out

Also in this issue »
WINTER 2009

€4.95 | £3.45 | ISSUE 21

IRENE KHAN
Amnesty International

BEYOND THE BOYS CLUB
Stepping Onto The Career Catwalk!

LIP SERVICE
It's All In The Packaging!

BOBBI BROWN
International Make-up Artist

ENTERING THE POLITICAL ARENA
Ivana Bacik Paves The Way!

VIVIENNE JUPP
A Zest For Life

WOMENMEANBUSINESS.COM

Winter 2009 issue of *WMB*.

Sarah Newman, founder of Needahotel.com, me and Sahar Hashemi, founder of Coffee Republic at the WMB Conference in 2009.

Phillip Matthews, president of the National College of Ireland and ex Ireland rugby captain – a big hit with the girls at our 2010 conference.

Me and Julie Meyer, founder of Ariadne Capital – WMB Conference 2010.

Summer 2011 issue of *WMB*.

Ronan Keating, me and Glenda Gilson enjoying a good read!

Autumn 2011 issue of *WMB*.

Our inaugural conference in Cork 2011, entitled 'Leadership & Women' – Sarah Newman, me, Mairead Maher, Kaye Ronayne, Jean van Sinderen-Law, Samantha McConnell and Maura Howe.

Although diamonds are a girl's best friend, cash is a girl's best asset in the times we live in.

I get quite hung up on cash flows – they are the lifeblood of a business, especially a young business. If we look at the companies that have closed their doors of late, we would find that this was probably down to two things – business had totally tapered off and/or they, even with sound orders on their books, ran out of cash. Cash flow is something I'm so cognisant of, and it amazes me to see so many people fail because they take their eye off the ball or lose perspective. Of course, they may be totally focused on their cash flows but just can't get the wherewithal from those fine banking institutions that not only screwed the country over once, but are now starving businesses of all-important credit facilities.

Loss of perspective caused our banking crisis – those who were meant to employ best practice, those who were supposed to monitor and regulate, took their eye off the ball and Mr Greed seized the opportunity. Now this once wonderful country that I was so proud of has to borrow heavily in order to stay afloat. We've literally run out of cash. We may have assets but they're not liquid, and if we go to sell our 'crown jewels' it's unlikely that we will realise anywhere near their value in the current climate. A country with no cash is a sitting duck.

There's little doubt that my Diploma in Applied Finance greatly helped me understand the need for cash flows. When I was moving up the career ladder, I was very focused on sales and targets and I wasn't always privy to the complete picture. The health of a company's cash is usually restricted to directors and shareholders, and, in a world where many women don't have access to the board-room, it's not surprising that they are shocked when it all comes tumbling down. Since this recession started, I have seen many amazing, talented women get their P.45. Accountants crunch the numbers, and talent and loyalty are replaced with cheaper models. However, it has also been my experience that talent isn't long out of a job. She may have to start over and prove herself, but she soon gains the respect and success that she deserves. It would be remiss of me not to mention my husband's contribution to my cash flow. He constantly brings me back to reality when I go off on one of my creative trips. He's my 'Steady Eddie' in every positive sense of the word. Entrepreneurs are visionaries and don't necessarily always think of the more practical aspects of business, tending to focus on the more creative side. I believe I'm both commercial and creative, which is really important as you need to wear a lot of Philip Treacy hats to succeed in today's cut-throat climate.

A simple exercise worth doing from the off is to find your breakeven point and work out your cash flow projections from there. Roughly work out all your overheads and divide them by twelve to see what monthly income you need to run a small, developing business over the year. It's simple arithmetic that gives you your 'must have' figure in an instant. Obviously there are many sophisticated financial models available for you to project your cash flows; I am merely letting you know what I did to give me a snapshot of my own situation when starting out. It's a simple yet sobering exercise. My breakeven figure scared the hell out of me.

There is plenty of free software available, even from the banks, which allows you to work out your cash flows. The trick is to get your income and expenditure accurate and then deliver. Five years ago, overheads were much higher than they are now. Rent, for instance, was anything between 20 and 40 per cent more. Just think of all those businesses that are in an upward-only lease review now. I'm not interested in long leases as I've always wanted to own my work space. However, it's one of those goals on my list that has dropped down the pecking order. Had I realised that particular objective, it would now be a noose around my hard neck.

A lot of my overheads have been trimmed down substantially as survival becomes the new 'success' story. Five years ago, I could not employ a good sales executive. Salaries at the time were averaging €50k plus, which for any new business was too much. Now I can find someone for half that. This does beg the question, though: if you are so tight on overheads and have limited human resources, how can you grow your brand and business without working yourself into an early grave? 'Mutual trading' has become the new model as businesses revert to trading standards of old, like the bartering system by which they trade their skills and services amongst one another. It can work well for a while but it doesn't pay the bills.

Probably one of the most important lessons I learned when I studied Marketing is the term 'opportunity cost'. In my case, I often need to stand back and decide what task to do next that would utilise my time best. In other words, how can I maximise on my services that generate the highest value of return to the company in the least time? The other lesson I learned early in business was to put a value on the brand called 'you'. Like me, many women set up their businesses in the service sector. Therefore, they not only need to know their breakeven point, they also need to put a realistic value on their time – their 'me' brand. The challenge is how do you re-value your time in the current marketplace, where many buyers are only interested in rock bottom quotes in return for a top quality service. I would argue that you need to really think about your opportunity cost. Only focus on projects that give you a fair return. If it means turning away business to avoid a race to the bottom, well, so be it. If you don't value your own time and service offered, why should you expect others to? It is very difficult to refuse work, especially now, but it is almost impossible to renegotiate once a price has been set – a loss leader* may

---

* A good example of a loss leader would be found in the supermarket sector where products are sold as 'special offers', probably at cost or even below cost in a bid to attract consumers who will inevitably buy other more profitable lines at the same time. It's a hook that reels in the potential customer or client. However, it is rarely the supermarket that pays the cost for these loss leaders; instead, this is put on the shoulders of the suppliers.

not lead to increased business in this environment.

I often have to think about the value of my time. I know that I undervalue my worth and this is primarily down to the fact that I don't pay myself what I'm worth. If you don't pay yourself your 'value', subconsciously you begin to believe that what you do pay yourself is what you're actually worth. Not a great place to be in, I can assure you. Research has shown that men put a greater value on themselves than women when setting up their business. But, hey, we already know that women get paid anything between 10 per cent and 17 per cent less than men for doing the same job! I believe most entrepreneurs, gender aside, would forego or reduce substantially their own income before letting one of their employees go. Perhaps it's a sense of responsibility or pride, but entrepreneurs tend to create cultures that are built on loyalty, trust and accountability.

Let's think for a moment about the 'me' brand. Next time you go to value a job, look at what you'd charge in 'normal' circumstances. Now discount this to allow for the extraordinary times we operate in and ensure that this discount doesn't drop below your breakeven point. Now that you have this figure, look at those companies who are most likely to value your expertise. The old adage 'pay peanuts, get monkeys' applies and, although some companies may risk reputation for short-term gain, it rarely leads to long-term rewards for their brand. I recall being put under increased pressure by a client to reduce a particular third-party service fee. Although I indicated that this was ill advised, I was put under continued pressure until I reluctantly agreed. As a result, I didn't get the service I needed, which had a knock-on effect on the project in hand. Of course, as the consultant, I couldn't and wouldn't go back to the client with the problem. I had to resolve the situation because, at the end of the day, I was the 'expert' engaged. Obviously I wasn't swayed when I was put under pressure to do this the next time – and there is always a next time. Lesson learned!

I recently set a new resolution for myself. It's quite cold and calculating but it is vital in order to succeed. I am not going to work on any projects (charity and networking aside) that doesn't involve a payment in return. In other words, I'm putting a value on *all* my business-related work. In a way, I'm cutting out the 'mutual trading', which was becoming more a norm than a necessity. In order to take this route, I need to offer a value added service while maintaining a reasonable fee. It does seem like a realistic goal and time will tell if I achieve it. However, I know that I need to consciously take this first step and make decisions based on the resolution before any real change can be seen.

The other goal I've set is to avoid time stealers. I'm sure you've come across these little gems on a daily basis. These can be dressed in suits or disguised as Mr or Ms Procrastination. The type of time stealers I experience in the fast-paced environment I work in include emails, unnecessary meetings and bumping into Mr or Ms Uncertainty. I'm sure there are plenty more but I think it best to identify the main ones, in my working life anyway.

Let's take meetings. It would be very unusual for me to request a meeting unless both parties had something to gain. Okay, this is somewhat subjective, but I'm assuming at this stage of my career that I know how to make a credible 'fit' between my brand and that of my potential client so that it's a 'win-win' situation for all. However, I do receive requests from total strangers to meet and usually it's a one-sided affair. These are the meetings that I'm learning to avoid and they do stand out a mile. Now, I have to accept that, in the game I'm in, many people will invariably look for publicity for their products and services. But there has to be a 'hook', a timely announcement, a newsworthy angle. Recently I was invited to LinkedIn by someone I didn't know. I accepted and before I knew it I was being invited to an event that totally infringed on my personal time (i.e. outside the acceptable office hours). I declined politely. Within a day or so, I received another request by said person to either write a profile on her or allow her to write a piece for the magazine. She was neither a writer nor a journalist. This is an example of a time stealer. She should have simply emailed, indicating what she needed and why I should consider her request. I like people who are open and candid. Unfortunately, as a nation we tend to beat around the bush too much. We also hate to say no, and tend to lead people down the garden path unnecessarily. I'm quite a direct person and I'm quick to make decisions. You could say that I prefer things to be black and white rather than grey. Not all my decisions are right, but I do tend to learn from my mistakes quickly. I also follow my gut if I'm finding a particular direction unclear. The gut is probably one of our greatest assets as women in business and, indeed, as mothers.

You become a great planner when you become a parent. In fact, everything you do comes down to time. One of the biggest mistakes employers make is to undervalue part-time working mums who wish to work and also address their family commitments. This breed of females not only know how to juggle various balls with precision but they also bring unique qualities to the table. They are time sensitive and therefore not time wasters. They love their role as parent but also value their opportunity to remain within a more flexible working environment. Yes, increased flexibility and understanding is necessary for such women, but I believe productivity increases when you have a tighter time frame. Game on.

Emails are probably one of the worst time stealers. In fact, technology has stretched us so far that our ability to really focus on a task, any task, has almost become a gift of yesteryear. Depending on which time management course you may have completed, you might be advised to avoid checking your emails first thing in the morning. Instead, you are recommended to look at your 'to do' list, which has been ordered in terms of priority and hopefully drawn up the night before. Any unnecessary distraction will take from what could be a productive workflow. Others will suggest that you should check your emails at around 11.00 a.m. so that you can address 'must do' items first and still keep abreast of new business. In the publishing industry, which relies so heavily on technology, I find that I always check my emails initially, but I've learned to only check the interesting ones before resuming my priority tasks. The subject field is so vital, as is the contact signature. Do you remember when you used to type a letter that was carbon backed? If you made a mistake, you either had to start again or go down the less professional 'Tipp-Ex' route. Then you had to put it into an envelope and stamp and post it. It might take three days for it to reach its final destination and another week before a response was received. However, even with this 'snail mail' method, big business was being done, empires were being built and millionaires were being made. So, I think it should be perfectly acceptable to allow yourself a day or so to review and respond to emails and to use the red 'urgent' flag if, and only if, it is indeed an urgent message for both you and your intended recipient.

Procrastination is not a problem of time management or poor planning. According to the great American entrepreneur Victor Kiam (who liked Remington Razors so much he bought the company), 'Procrastination is opportunity's assassin.' I don't regard myself as a procrastinator. I do, however, see this trait in my business encounters, which has the knock-on effect of wasting my time. You will know Mr or Ms Procrastination when you meet them. This is the type of individual who actively looks for distractions; who is afraid of failure and sometimes of success; who avoids making any meaningful or enlightening decisions lest he or she has to take responsibility for the outcome. Inevitably, this individual extinguishes team spirit in a working environment. Yes, procrastination is something I strenuously avoid in my own life and it certainly helps to recognise the traits in yourself and others.

So now that we have identified time stealers and have a fair idea of our cash flow requirements, how do we grow our businesses in the strait jacket of our less-than-booming economy? Answer: with lots of determination, an element of risk and an ability to see an opportunity. When I started out, I had a slush fund – money set aside for investment in the business when needed. Most of this funding went into building up the brand, covering overheads like staff and other necessities. They do say you have to 'speculate to accumulate'. However, a lesson I learned late in the process, which should have been as obvious as the nose on my face, was the lack of commercial accountability I had applied to each staff member. Now, I know sales people are a breed onto themselves, but if you have a small team who don't play an active daily role in the commercial operation of your business, well, they are a drain on your purse. Yes, they could be talented, creative and personable, but without the ability to see an opportunity for new business, without a value-added slant to their role, dare I say it, they are dispensable. What I should have been looking for were commercial animals above creative ones.

For the first eighteen months or so, business was really taking off and I had big plans for the WMB brand. It was well received by the media, public and corporate Ireland. We had a whole world to conquer and were still at the tail end of the Celtic tiger economy. It wasn't surprising, therefore, that we showed a profit that for any business in its infancy was a great achievement. Although I was always stretched, as I was working with limited human and financial resources, it was a positive and motivated atmosphere. I have always said that if you gave me a blank cheque, I probably wouldn't have achieved what I did without one. When you're operating in a start-up business, you tend to be more creative and 'think outside the box' in order to get around obstacles. And, let's face it, there are daily challenges in any new set-up. For instance, my blank cheque may have provided me with a state-of-the-art premises, something that I had always enjoyed previously. The alternative was for me to use my aunt's empty house, which saved on rent. I think you get the picture. You cut your cloth to suit and there's no room for egos or notions of grandeur.

Towards the end of year two, however, negative economic news was beginning to filter through the business world. My slush fund was depleting at a ferocious rate as my cash flows came under increased pressure. It was easy to see what was happening. Advertising plans were being put on hold; I still had to pay the staff and the rent; I still was a new business driving brand awareness. In year three the vista changed dramatically as our economy imploded. I had set myself the goal of reaching breakeven by the end of the year. You can imagine my disappointment as I saw my figures nosedive. You do question what you're doing and where you're going under these circumstances. You reassess what's important to you – your family, your health, your relationships, your self-worth. I know I had a good cry (in private), I dusted myself back down, held my head up high and off I went again in the direction of destiny. It's this tenacity that separates leaders from followers and I have it in abundance.

So my three-year plan went out the window, followed by the old cash flows and budgets. I decided year four would be my new year three and I would have to make some hard decisions in order to survive to breakeven and beyond. Most sectors of my business plan were delivering apart from the magazine. This wasn't in itself surprising as creating a title takes years and deep pockets. I had neither, only buckets of enthusiasm and belief. My limited resources meant that I was finishing a magazine in one month and starting the sales and editorial process for the next issue immediately afterwards. You can cope with this situation for a while but eventually you don't have time to plan ahead or seek out new opportunities; you have no time to think.

I looked at *WMB* magazine, which was bi-monthly, and made the decision to go quarterly. It was the best decision that I made and *WMB* wouldn't be around today otherwise. Okay, the alternative would have been to find an investor, maintain my bi-monthly status and employ more staff – a high-risk strategy, given what was coming down the line. I guess I wanted to sink or swim on my own merit and, although they say 'pride comes before a fall', I would say it wasn't pride that got me through but experience. By going quarterly, I was still able to produce a great product but I also had the time to work on other projects in a more strategic way. This decision helped my cash flows considerably and, although it would reduce the growth of the printed medium, it allowed expansion in other, more profitable areas of my business. I also didn't need, for example, a full-time graphic designer. My designer at the time wanted to move out of the city for a better quality of life without the commute as she was expecting her first child. I was able to improve my cash flows and today she still designs *WMB* magazine on a freelance basis. Yes, I had to change my work flow; yes, I had to get my head around not having someone sitting at their desk at arm's length; and, yes, there were periods of panic. With the magazine running on a much tighter footing, I knew I was building a brand organically. Quality was still paramount and it's one thing I've never compromised on. By 2010, I had steadied the ship, which would have sank like so many others if I hadn't changed path and monitored the money closely. I reached breakeven, which was two years later than planned. But, as I said earlier, survival is the new success these days.

Belief is one of the best tools you can have in order to succeed. I remember planning my cash flows for year four and, as I considered my possible income and outgoings, I looked at the probable end result and I didn't like what I saw. There was far too much red and not enough black. I had put so much effort (and money) into the business and I wasn't going to allow it (or me) to fail, although that's exactly what was staring me in the face. I recalled something that Jack Black had reiterated in one of his workshops – 'Don't set realistic goals; set bold goals.' After all, realistic goals must, by their very nature, be achievable. My projected cash flows would only send me in the direction of disaster. So I revised my goals. I increased my turnover against a very bleak economic backdrop. I left very little room for manoeuvre on my overheads. I didn't know exactly where I was going to get the increased business. All I knew was that I had to find it, whether it was more ads in the magazine, more sponsors of the Awards or more contract publishing. At least I had avenues to explore. Once I committed my projections to paper, I had already sealed the deal. It was now the job of sheer belief and hard work to realise the results, and that's exactly what happened.

However, as much as strong belief can deliver positive actions and results, its nemesis doubt can play tricks with your thoughts. Doubt can bring great uncertainty, which leads to negative thinking and outcomes. It usually comes in the darkest moments. It creeps up on you in the middle of the night, interrupting your sleep as you toss and turn, wrestling with its shadow. I sometimes wake in the morning in a troubled state with doom lurking in my mind. And as I shower away the cobwebs of doubt, I think about how far I've come and begin to believe again. Such are the roller-coaster emotions of this entrepreneur and, I'm sure, of most entrepreneurs. The trick is to fight the pangs of negativity and keep as balanced and positive an outlook as possible. The great thing about cash flows is that, graphically, they can quickly show where you are leaking. As bank charges increase and overdraft facilities become more costly, it's vital to stay within your means whenever possible. Publishing revenues, by their very nature, can be somewhat unpredictable, whereas overheads are remorselessly constant. I had noticed a trend year-on-year that the first quarter was always tough, with little cash coming in. However, with my new quarterly magazine deadlines, there was a gap in our work schedules that we could fill if I could only find an opportunity. Now, I was already doing contract work, I already hosted our very successful annual Conference & Awards in Dublin and I was working on our Internet strategy. However, I had a desire to run events around the country as I believed the demand was there. This kind of departure is where a certain amount of risk and belief is necessary, probably in equal amounts.

I decided to run our first mini-conference outside of the capital in the lovely city of Cork in April 2011. I wanted to provide real value and access to a motivational experience, all within a positive networking environment. As a national publication, *WMB* could bring coverage, attract good-calibre sponsors, appeal to business-women and female entrepreneurs, and provide a professional event. The return for me would be that extra bit of business to plug my first-quarter cash flows. I guess, before now, I wasn't really open to considering this opportunity, although I always had the desire to host a Cork event. How it came about was all about timing, though. In 2010, a Cork woman had won the WMB Businesswoman of the Year Award, which, given that she was in the educational sector, was a unique achievement. Jean van Sinderen-Law is director of development at University College Cork; she possesses an innate ability to transcend the learning and educational sector and illustrate her role as a vital business function which connects the disciplines of education and business very successfully. It wasn't long before Jean and I got talking about WMB coming to Cork. Opportunity knocked and I answered her door willingly. I lined up serial entrepreneur Sarah Newman as the keynote speaker.

There's always a certain amount of risk in any new project and I weighed up the actual cost to host the event against the likely seat sales and sponsor income. There's big money to be made in speaking engagements, if you're the actual speaker! I'm of the view that women rarely book an event just because of the speaker. Yes, he or she is an important part of the offering, but usually there's another hook like networking, which is the overriding attraction, especially in recent years when building contacts has become vital for business survival and success.

A lot of negotiation is involved when booking your speaker and an agent can make or break a deal. It also takes quite a while to find the 'right' speaker and, once I have my mind set on a particular person, no one else will do. I recall the previous year when I wanted to book Julie Meyer for our conference in Dublin. Julie's credentials are top notch – she has been named one of INSEAD's top 50 Alumni; Ernst & Young Entrepreneur of the Year; World Economic Forum Global Leader of Tomorrow. She is among the *TIME* magazine Digital 50 and is one of the Top 30 Most Influential Women in Europe. I therefore knew she was going to cost. Karren Brady, Lord Sugar's right-hand woman on *The Apprentice*, had given me details of an agent in the UK who might be able to help. Julie was available, but the agency was looking for payment up front. Of course, this was all in the small print and fortunately I had asked for their terms and conditions in advance of signing. Paying a substantial fee up front would have played havoc with my cash flows. In addition, I would be literally bankrolling a UK agent months in advance for no reason. I don't have a problem putting a deposit down for services but I certainly wouldn't agree to their conditions. I ended up directly booking Julie Meyer for our Conference & Awards. It is always best to go direct, but not always possible. Lesson learned.

Fortunately, for our Cork conference, I had a track record with Sarah Newman so there was a certain trust and professionalism from the off. Speaker booked, I now needed to identify those sponsors who would benefit from an involvement in a high-calibre event targeted at businesswomen and female entrepreneurs. I had already set the theme as 'Leadership and Women', which was topical and relevant. I wanted to secure three sponsors who could cover our overheads; the seat costs would cover the third party costs such as speakers, audio-visual, branding, etc. It's quite amazing how you can get the runaround from some potential clients and how others just 'get it' straight away. When dealing with potential clients, always ensure that you've identified the decision maker in the process – it cuts out time and endless frustration.

All the while I was organising our inaugural Cork event, we were also putting an issue of *WMB* to bed. Of course, I wanted to promote the event, the sponsors and the speakers in the issue. No matter how well you plan, it always comes down to the wire. As I approached our deadline, I was still chasing commitments, copy and sign-off. At a certain point in a project's planning, there is what I can best describe as a 'tipping point' – a balancing act where you need to carefully line up all the balls and, if one or two drop off, well, you're royally screwed! It's a delicate phase and you have to keep a clear focus and a strong belief, otherwise you'll fall into a panic. The adage 'Fail to prepare; prepare to fail' comes to mind. Of all the traits I have inherited from my father, it is my ability to plan and to ensure I have a backup plan.

There are a number of elements you need to ensure a successful event – the theme has to be relevant and unique; the speakers have to be top drawer; the venue has to be accessible and enticing; the pricing has to be right; and, most importantly, you need to have access to your market (in my case, businesswomen and female entrepreneurs). All boxes ticked, I set my target for 150+ attendees. Having the magazine printed and speakers and sponsors on board was only half the battle. The task of getting bums on seats proved, as it often does, to be arduous. It provided for a rollercoaster of mixed emotions as I hit and missed my daily targets. I can safely say that, although I enjoy event management, I would have little interest in doing it full time.

Potential disaster struck when, within a week of launching our event, Sarah Newman was making headlines for all the wrong reasons. A business she was involved in with her partner DJ Carey was in deep financial trouble. This was not something that I had anticipated. I kept my head and kept the faith – after all, Sarah had spoken at one of our previous events and she was top drawer. Then it dawned on me that, despite her own personal and perceived wealth, which had been realised by the purchase of her company Needahotel.com some years earlier, this latest news story just highlighted the extraordinary times that we *all* live and operate in. It is this ability to look for the real story, the real angle, that separates destiny from disaster. Sarah told her story – warts and all.

Our Cork event was a tremendous success. I'm a great believer in karma and that you will always get back what you put in. So believe.

Chapter 8

Waistlines and Deadlines

The Yo-Yo Diet of a Stressed Businesswoman

'There's a 25-stone girl living inside me who wants to get out, but I just try to keep her in!'

Dr Eva Orsmond, Orsmond Clinics and panellist on RTÉ's *Operation Transformation*; interviewed in *WMB*, issue 18

Month: August
Thought: Get a top-to-toe health check.

I T WAS JULY 2007 and I was on the phone to my brother Michael. He had just told me to sit down. 'You need to sit down,' he said. 'Is there someone with you?' I didn't quite know why I needed someone with me. 'It's Paul. It's bad news. I don't think he's going to make it.'

I sat down, the receiver shaking in my hand. 'What do you mean he's not going to make it?'

'I've just got the call. You know as much as me. He's probably gone.'

'You mean he's dead?'

'Yes, I think so.'

'Jesus, Michael, is he dead? What exactly have you been told?'

I eventually put down the receiver and began to shake incessantly. My brother Paul had been in France on holidays. He had just been promoted to Lieutenant Colonel some months previously. He was only forty-nine. The tragedy had such similarities to my father's passing. Both father and son were high achievers who thrived on stress, but unfortunately their hearts were not as strong as their desire to succeed.

It's difficult when someone with so much to live for is suddenly taken. Death forces people to reflect on their lives in different ways. It has a rippling effect, as family and friends come to terms with the immediate loss and the ensuing realisation that they could be next. I had learned to live with death from an early age: first, my father; then a number of young friends; then my mother. And now my brother. I found it comforting to know that, as a family, we had all been together just four months previously at my wedding celebrations. I know I would have found Paul's death far more difficult if I hadn't had this time with him and with the family as a whole.

It dawned on me that, as with my father, I had a lot more in common with my brother than I had previously thought. We shared the same drive and work ethic, which was somewhat balanced with a gregarious disposition. Four years have passed since I received that phone call. In the meantime, I have been poked and prodded by consultants and specialists to ensure that I don't travel the same road. Like my father and my brother, I rise to the challenges of stressful situations; I purposely put myself beyond my comfort zone in order to grow. I am a born leader with oodles of energy and my mind never switches off. Yes, I relax; yes, I have a laugh. But I'm always thinking, strategising, dreaming – It's what makes me tick.

I thrive on stress, but at the cost of my health. Keeping fit and trim is something I just can't measure up to. We're a family of foodies – we love our food and the odd drink. We have to work at keeping fit with varying degrees of success, and cholesterol remains our best friend despite all our efforts. Even the most agile of us needs to pop the daily dosage of costly medicines that supposedly keep the bad cholesterol at bay. I rarely find the time to exercise and I'm totally allergic to the 'D' word. Even the thought of dieting depresses me. My waistline expands and decreases depending on how stressed I am. I'm a hypochondriac who has all the symptoms but who is never really sick.

Our successful entrepreneurs seem to have the perfect waistlines to go with their more-than-perfect bottom lines. Looking at some of our successful female role models, they seem to have it all – the loot, the looks and the long legs. Perhaps attractive people attract success – now, there's a thought. I like to think I'm more akin to Oprah Winfrey, who has always struggled with her weight. I'm prepared to be less perfect, if I can follow in her footsteps!

I wasn't always so fickle about my health. In school I could eat all around me and not put on a single ounce. It helps when you're running up and down a basketball court daily. Then I discovered the social scene, abandoned the world of routine and my waistline expanded to accommodate my new lifestyle. It's always been a goal of mine to get healthier, to lose weight, to be that perfect size 12. But the goal somehow manages to drop down the list of priorities. When you are juggling so many balls, you tend to leave your own needs until last or perhaps until it's too late. The yo-yo diet of businesswomen is just that – as we strive to be the supportive wife, caring mother, motivating employer and best friend, we sometimes forget about ourselves and our health.

My name is Rosemary Delaney and I'm a walking health risk. There, I've said it. Now, let's do something about it.

There are ways to measure stress and, indeed, link stress to subsequent illness. The Holmes and Rahe Stress Scale measures a number of 'life change units' that apply to events in an individual's life over a period of time, which, when added together, give a rough estimate of how stress affects your health. So, if I take my brother's death (63 units), add this to my recent marriage (50 units) and top this up with business re-adjustments (39 units), my total for these three stresses alone amounts to 152 units. According to the Holmes and Rahe Stress Scale, this puts me in the 'Risk of illness is moderate' category. The top ten high-scoring life events that can play havoc with your stress levels include: death of a spouse (understandably, 100 units); divorce (73); marital separation (65); imprisonment (63); death of a close family member (63); personal injury or illness (53); marriage (50); dismissal from work (47); marital reconciliation (43); and, finally, retirement (45).

Stress can be positive or negative. I live with both. The recession has brought increased health risks to businesses, young and old. As the line between our personal and professional lives become blurred, we struggle to meet deadlines and become overly obsessed with bottom lines in the name of survival. These tensions are the ingredients for a perfect health scare – on top of a family history like mine, they can be lethal.

Three years ago, I was driving to a meeting down the country and had tuned into the late Gerry Ryan, who happened to be interviewing a guy called Michael O'Doherty. It wasn't long before I was transfixed by the conversation, which went on for some forty minutes. O'Doherty had co-founded a company called Plexus Bio-Energy; to many, he was known as a 'healer'. He has written a number of books, the latest being *Just Imagine*. His passion and conviction for what he does was all-consuming and I knew in an instant that I had to find out more about his philosophy on using energy to manage health and healing.

He described various symptoms and emotions brought on by

stress and other more serious illnesses. I realised that I was that person he was describing who suffered from upset stomachs, poor diet, fluctuating energy levels and an overactive imagination. Within the week, I had convinced him to speak at WMB's Conference & Awards. I even took a weekend out of my schedule to learn more about bio-energy therapy at his two-day workshop.

For centuries, scientists, researchers and medical professionals have been searching for cures to various ailments and disorders. Many previously fatal conditions have been eradicated only to be replaced by even more deadly forces. As our world becomes supposedly more sophisticated, why are cancers, heart attacks, strokes and other life-threatening conditions on the increase? Is there just too much chaos and stress in our world or are we missing the bigger picture?

O'Doherty's theory is quite simple. Each of us is made up of energy. Bio-energy simply means life energy. However, if the bio-energetic structure of our body becomes imbalanced in any way, the body becomes unwell. For the body to recover, you have to work at this bio-energy level. O'Doherty has developed a host of techniques to manipulate the energetic system and to scan the energy field of your body. If blockages are found, they can be released through a series of actions to re-balance and re-establish the flow of energy to the body. Once the flow is re-established, the intelligence encased is what allows the body to heal. Part of the process is to learn to breathe properly and to look at diet and exercise. But the energy needs to get flowing properly.

For two decades, O'Doherty has been practising what he preaches. He rose to prominence when he successfully treated *Lord of the Dance* star Michael Flatley, who had been struck down with a virus that caused him to cancel a world tour. Flatley openly attributed his remarkable recovery to O'Doherty's healing hands. Hoping to get a few tips on coping with stress, I asked O'Doherty if there was indeed such a thing as positive stress or were we all doomed. He explained to me that stress has an impact on the body and sometimes what happens is we adapt to that stress. However, by adapting, we start developing symptoms – tiredness, digestive disorders, back pain, fatigue – and eventually this leads to adrenal function problems or burnout – sound familiar? When your adrenal functions are affected, you end up with a lot of symptoms and often your production capability at work just doesn't exist.

If you are aware of the hazards associated with your job, you can take steps to understand and prevent stress – it doesn't have to manifest as a disease. According to O'Doherty, it's a question of mind influencing matter. Our thoughts, our feelings and our perceptions influence our body's physiology. If we have a thought, a feeling or a perception that our disease is going to kill us – we're right. If we have a feeling, a thought or a perception that what we have can be cured – we're right. That's the way the body works. We need to therefore understand that health isn't a miraculous thing; it's a natural thing. It's natural to be healthy; it's not natural to be sick. Sickness is an unnatural reaction to a natural state and we have to look at our natural state.

I have dipped in and out of 'perfect' balance and I'm coming to the realisation that stress is very much a part of my life. I just need to recognise its symptoms and be more proactive in managing them. Breathing exercises, meditation and a positive belief system can help combat stressful situations or phases. I have also put diet and exercise as priorities on my goals list. By doing this, I have re-evaluated what is important at this current time. I only have to look at my young daughter too get the impetus to succeed in my endeavours. I remember only too well what it was like to lose a parent at such a young age.

Seven months down the line of putting my health front-of-mind, I have lost over nine kilogrammes in weight. One day when I was at a low ebb, I filled a very large canvas bag with food – all the things I had cut down and, indeed, cut out. The objective of the exercise was to ensure that the bag had to be equal to the weight I had lost – I could barely lift it. This visual exercise clearly showed me how far I had come in such a short time. It gave me the motivation to continue on my road to perfect health. On my journey, I have met many women who have faced serious health risks with varying degrees of success. I recall working with one woman who was full of life and passion for what she did. One year she was working with me at one of our events, the next year she was battling with cancer. The following year she had tragically lost her brave fight. Another very successful businesswoman described how she had battled with breast cancer. She fortunately survived her ordeal, while coping with a young child and a demanding career. In fact, soon after getting the all-clear, she refocused her energy to attain a fantastic promotion. There are literally thousands of stories of how people have overcome health issues, many brought on by stressful situations and a poor diet and exercise regime.

In an effort to combat stress, or at least learn to cope with it, I have devised the WMB Ten Stress-Busting Tips to keep you in harmony when all those nail-biting moments creep up on you. They are based on experience, rather than science, and are just some ways that I have learned to be more proactive.

WMB Ten Stress-Busting Tips

1. Reflection
Our current economic situation has forced all of us to stretch ourselves even more. As businesses cut their staffing levels in order to stay afloat, there is little room for manoeuvre. Those left behind express feelings of relief tempered with frustration. You not only have to be as good as your last deal, you now have to be better. Projects take twice as long to complete, because clients demand twice as much. The atmosphere is constantly changing

as battles are won, and lost. The pressure is on and you must rise to the challenge repeatedly.

Perhaps, instead of looking at where you are now, reflect on how far you have come. Seldom is acknowledgement bestowed on us for a job well done – such are the crisis management roles many of us find ourselves taking on. But you can pat yourself on the back and acknowledge how far you have come on your journey and how much you have achieved. I recall speaking to an audience of female entrepreneurs and I asked them to take a moment and literally pat themselves on the back. They had survived the cull, and they needed to acknowledge this great feat. They bashfully laughed, they patted, then they understood. Lesson learned.

2. Balance

Getting the work–life balance right is a somewhat clichéd debate. Balance implies a state of equilibrium and I have, as yet, to meet a person who exudes this aura of perfection. As I attempted to balance my private and professional life, I began to notice that all I was doing was stressing myself out. On one hand, I wanted to be a domestic goddess and, on the other, a publishing diva – all I was achieving was half-baked cupcakes on the back of half-finished project plans.

I recall attending a networking event and sitting at a table of strangers. We were having a discussion about our challenges and, as I heard myself speak, my little inner voice was saying the words, 'This is it. Learn to live with it.' Another more seasoned business-woman at the table piped up to inform me that the life of an entrepreneur doesn't get any easier – it's the path we choose.

I decided from that point that I would not strive for balance but would learn to accept with open arms the positive state of imbalance. Yes, I would have deadlines to meet and, during these hectic periods, the house would look like a tip and I wouldn't be able to bake like I love to. Equally, when I had less pressure on, I could linger in the classroom when dropping my daughter to school and I could indulge my *MasterChef* aspirations.

3. Exercise

I'm haphazard at exercise. Despite having two dogs and a fabulous park facility nearby, I always make excuses. I'm usually too busy or just too tired to get those walking shoes on. All of us are time poor. However, we know that the more exercise we get, the more energy we have. I've done two things to rectify the status quo. During the finer months, I leave the car at home on at least two days in the week. I am therefore 'forced' to take the Luas, and to walk the twenty minutes to the stop in the morning and back in the evening. If everyone decided to take this initiative, not only would they be healthier but they would also satisfy their 'green' conscience. Job done. For the not-so-nice evenings, I have invested in a cross trainer and, five out of seven nights, I do twenty minutes' exercise, which equates to 7 kilometres or 160 calories lost. When you do this, and see how much sweat it takes to work off 160 calories, you soon question that little biscuit that's saying 'Eat me'! I can confirm that the more I exercise, the better I feel. It releases all that pent-up emotion and unwanted stress from the day's happenings.

4. Awareness

If you go into the office each day, you probably tend to dress according to the company culture. Therefore, when you come home, it's a good idea to change out of your work clothes into something more relaxing. Basically, you're shifting your mood and acknowledging that you're now in a different, more stress-free space. If you, like many, now work remotely from home, it's vital that you get into an appropriate routine. Don't linger in your dressing-gown just because you can. Ensure your office space at home is sufficient to allow you to function efficiently and effectively. Avoid positioning your chair with your back to the door and ensure there's plenty of natural light. Be aware of time but not overtly so.

I have never used an alarm clock to get up. In fact, Jack Black, founder of MindStore, teaches people who attend his programmes how to live without this 'alarming' device. It has been an accepted ritual by millions over the decades to actually be awoken out of a deep sleep with a jolt – not a great way to kick-start the day and even, I would say, rather stressful.

5. Planning

It's amazing how little basic planning we do. I'm always disappointed by the lack of goal setting that goes on around me. I'm not suggesting for one moment that people have to strive for greatness, but they should aim for those goals that will give them a more fulfilling and happy life. As demands for our time increase tenfold, it's the omission of the little details that can sometimes scupper the bigger picture. Each evening before you finish work, plan the next day and commit your plan to paper. Prioritise those tasks that need to be done and ensure that you've allowed yourself enough leeway to complete them. Technology can be your best friend when planning. As I type this book on my laptop, I can access my office computer by remote dial up. I'm also surrounded by my other gadgets: my iPhone, which is as much a part of my handbag as my credit cards, and my wonderful iPad. All help me connect, all help to organise my day, if used appropriately. Avoid those time stealers (e.g. constantly checking your emails and Twitter) and you'll avoid unnecessary stress and distraction.

6. PMA – The Opposite of PMT!

A positive mental attitude is something that you may have inherently. For those not so lucky, you can develop this trait once you become aware of its effectiveness. Each morning I routinely ask my young daughter if she has everything – her homework, lunch-box and her positive mental attitude. She has a lively disposition and always cracks a laugh. In fact, she wakes up singing. Her positivity is contagious. Not only is it important for you to recognise and nurture this positivity in yourself, but you also need to ensure that you surround yourself with like-minded individuals. We all know the adage 'Life is too short', so don't make it any shorter by allowing others to stress you out. A positive mental attitude is one that sees the glass half full, not half empty. It comes into play when you look at a problem and see an opportunity.

Napoleon Hill, author of *Think and Grow Rich*, identifies the seven major positive emotions – desire, faith, love, sex, enthusiasm, romance and hope. Set against these positive emotions, he also identifies the seven major negative emotions which need to be avoided – fear, jealousy, hatred, revenge, greed, superstition and anger. In a world that displays so many of the latter traits, we need more people who will embrace positivity and spread it like the honey bee spreads pollen.

I absolutely believe that positive thoughts bring positive things. It's probably easier to demonstrate the converse as we see so many people fall into decline when surrounded by negativity – just look at the effects of greed on our economy. People who have a positive mental attitude, and I would put myself into this category, don't go around in denial like Eleanor H. Porter's fictional Pollyanna, but they do have a 'can-do' attitude and will seek out positive options to deliver positive results in difficult circumstances. Your mind has a secret talisman, so tap into it.

7. News Blackout

Let's face it, you rarely see good news hit the headlines. We're bombarded by news through so many avenues – radio, news-papers, TV, RSS feeds and various social networking channels.

Unfortunately, as serious crimes such as murder and rape become more the norm than the exception, we become somewhat desensitised. As we read about tsunamis, earthquakes, war and famine, we thank our lucky stars that it's not on our own doorsteps. But look at what is – human trafficking, paedophile rings and gangland slayings.

News is obviously important from the point of view of understanding the society in which we live. It is important to be informed. And since I work in the media, it would be difficult to abide by a news curfew anyway. However, news should be digested at a rate that is acceptable to your own well-being. I have often read stories, especially those to do with neglect or abuse of children, that send tears rolling down my cheeks. Empathy is a positive human trait. However, overdosing on news can cause anxiety and increased negativity. Continuous over-exposure is a recipe for disaster.

8. Passionate Pursuits

Although time is a scarce commodity these days, and we may struggle to give time to things not work- or family-related, it is good to remember that taking time for your health is a worthy thing to do. I find that, when I'm in the thick of so many projects and deadlines, it's important to be able to take a step back in order to find the impetus to move forward again. A walk in a leafy park can bring you closer to nature and to a more balanced state of being; a brush and blank canvas can inspire your visual senses; an impromptu spa treatment can unlock the aches and pains of a stressful and demanding schedule. I'm a confirmed shopaholic and nothing beats a morning of retail therapy followed by a leisurely lunch. It all sounds perfectly decadent, but when you work hard you also need to occasionally be good to yourself – after all, you're worth it!

9. Motivational Messaging

Over the years, I've come across some great authors and speakers, people who seem to have a unique window into life. I've already touched on Jack Black's MindStore and Napoleon Hill's *Think and Grow Rich*. Hill also co-wrote a book with W. Clement Stone entitled *Success through a Positive Mental Attitude*. He introduces the work with the line: 'The greatest secret of success is: there's no secret' (p.17). I've been touched by Randy Pausch's *Last Lecture*, James Redfield's *Celestine Prophecy* and Eckhart Tolle's spiritually enlightening *The Power of Now*. However, inspirational soundings can come from closer quarters, provided we open our ears – and minds – to hear them. As a woman in business, I was inspired when Mary Robinson said: 'I was elected by the women of Ireland, who, instead of rocking the cradle, rocked the system.' Motivational messaging is all around us, provided we are tuned into its airwaves.

10. Meditation

A recent study led by a team of Harvard-affiliated researchers at Massachusetts General Hospital has documented meditation-produced changes over time in regions of the brain associated with memory, sense of self, empathy and stress. The study's senior author Sara Lazar, a Harvard Medical School instructor in Psychology, referred to the common link between meditation and a sense of peacefulness and physical relaxation, but also demonstrated possible cognitive and psychological benefits. This is all good news, as I, for one, would be happy to improve my memory capabilities while decreasing my stress levels.

For me, meditation is visiting a peaceful place that quietens the brain and allows total rest. It's escapism of sorts. I use visualism, a form of seeing something clearly in my mind. I think of somewhere that I have visited in my past – a place where I have felt totally at one with nature. I remember taking a trip to

Kylemore Abbey on the shore of a lake in Connemara in the West of Ireland almost a decade ago. As I walked around the grounds, I came upon a little bench on a small, shingled inlet. As I sat there, I was aware of the birds chirping cheerfully in the trees all around the shimmering blue lake. The water darted through the stones beneath my feet and I sat in total amazement at the beauty and tranquility of the setting. When I meditate I am transported back to that exact setting on that warm summer's afternoon. It lifts my spirits and banishes stress from my system in an instant.

We all need to find these memories, these episodes in time, that allow us to feel totally content and at peace. Achieving this state can take time and effort and you may find you want some help with the process. Jack Black of MindStore teaches how to achieve this state of mind. Many people who practise yoga enter a similarly calm state of mind. Meditation, visualisation – call it what you will. We all need to positively connect with nature and with our souls.

Chapter 9

Role Models
They Come in Different Sizes!

'It is always important to be true to your innate values because if people believe in you they will be willing to follow you as a leader. Being believable is important.'

— **Cathriona Hallahan, managing director, Microsoft European Operations Centre; WMB Businesswoman of the Year 2009**

Month: September
Thought: Live beyond your comfort zone.

THE WORD 'COMFORT' conjures up a host of feelings. As children, we enjoyed the protective blanket of parental love and the comforts of our home, secure in the knowledge that we belonged. There were no huge demands, no major hurdles to jump, just acceptance of our surrounds and a naïve belief that we could be whatever we wanted to be. Time brings transformation as we begin to find our own way in life – still with the underlying desire to rekindle those feelings of comfort we had in our youth. The adage 'History repeats itself' rings true as we begin to sound just like our mothers and understand that the generation gap will always exist, no matter how trendy we think we are, or how tuned in. However, I believe that, in order to fulfil your dreams and desires, you need to place yourself outside this happy continuity, outside of the familiar, outside of your comfort zone, so that you can stretch and grow.

> 'If you always do what you always did, you'll always get what you always got.' **(Anon.)**

I do wonder what really motivates me, what pushes me that bit more. Is it the desire for success, for monetary gain? Perhaps it's the wish to make a difference and give back to society, or maybe my capacity to sink or swim on my own merits. Yes, I'm a 'lipstick entrepreneur' with plenty of attitude, who is willing to discard the familiar in search of the new. Success, my friends, always lurks just beyond your comfort zone. You can see it; you can taste it. You just need to want it enough to venture forth.

> **'Lipstick entrepreneurs':** I came across this term two years ago when Avon Cosmetics (with the Federation of Small Businesses) released some interesting research entitled: *The Rise of the Lipstick Entrepreneurs*. It demonstrates how the recession has acted as a catalyst for exponential growth in female-owned start-up businesses and predicts an increase of 100 per cent more female enterprises (FMEs) in the next decade (we'll have to wait and see). The report uncovers that, not for the first time in history, the economic crisis has powered the progression of women. Anna Segatti, president of Avon UK & Ireland (interviewed in *WMB*, issue 25) believes: 'The Lipstick Entrepreneur has discovered she can have it all – balancing her family needs with her ambitious business goals. However, more support for other women to ride the "Femterprise wave" is needed...'.

The social and economic drivers behind the rise of lipstick entrepreneurs are expected to result in a wider feminisation of business and society. These drivers include the Internet, which has made it possible for women to set up micro-enterprises and/or work from home in a way that was impossible in the past. The flexible benefits of being your own boss has also encouraged the growth of 'femterprise'.

The Avon-commissioned report identifies eight different types of lipstick entrepreneur: the Meritocrat – opted out of a successful career to strike out on her own; the Rescuer – stepped up to protect her family's finances; the Horizontal Juggler – excels in all areas of her life; the Double Hitter – runs her own business around another full-time job; the Domestecutive – works from home so she can juggle work and family; the Passionista – followed her passion and turned a hobby into a business; the Fledgling – self-employed school leaver or graduate; and the Freewheeler – approaching or beyond retirement age.

Which one are you?

My route to entrepreneurship tells me I'm a Meritocrat with a desire to be a Horizontal Juggler, but falling short. It's a bit like that question that groups of women have often asked each other: which *Sex and the City* character are you? We all perhaps admire Samantha – the independent, sassy dominatrix. But she can be just that bit too familiar at the best of times. We can identify with Carrie – the creative, confident, career-focused gal who is always on the edge of love. I know a lot of women remind me of Miranda – way too opinionated but well meaning. Finally, Charlotte – the socialite who lives in fairyland and occasionally hops on the roller-coaster of reality. So, which kind of lipstick do you wear – blush red like a beacon, or light rose, subtle yet sublime?

Businesswomen and female entrepreneurs are my target market for *WMB*. However, so too are those women who have probably spent the last decade or so of their lives rearing their offspring, having put their careers on the back burner. What's a woman supposed to do when her children no longer depend on her? I can only imagine how my own mother must have felt when the last child left the comforts of her nest. I was that child and it was a very hard and emotional period in our lives. I knew I wanted to see the world, to experience life outside the sleepy village I came from. But with that desire came the realisation that I would hurt her considerably. After all, my mother had different plans for me. History will repeat itself when my own daughter takes flight. In the meantime, I'll embrace her dreams as if they are my own. My target market also includes the tug-of-war mum who works part time, trying to get the balance of work and motherhood right and perhaps often feeling only half in control. Then there's the lifestyle entrepreneur, who creates her business around her family, and the mainstream entrepreneur, who plans her family around her working life. The common bond that connects us is a desire to grow – an ability to step outside our comfort zones on a daily basis.

I have enormous respect for stay-at-home mums. I think it is one of the hardest jobs in the world. I'm sure they, in turn, wonder how mums working outside of the home manage to complete their 'paid tasks' along with home responsibilities. I'd like to digress a little, if I may, as I think it's worth taking time to put a monetary value on the work we do in the home. Last year, insurers Caledonian Life released some findings that put an approximate price tag on the work of the stay-at-home parent. Their motive may have been to sell more personal insurance cover perhaps, but the facts remain. The study detailed the costs that would be incurred to employ someone to undertake the typical household jobs carried out by the stay-at-home mum or dad (more likely to be the former). These costs would be significant and, in many cases, unaffordable for families to sustain in the event of the homemaker's demise. Caledonian Life identified eleven major jobs that a typical homemaker might perform at home, such as housekeeper, cook, child minder and tutor, and the number of hours they typically devoted to each of those duties. They then determined the competitive market value that an employer would pay for one person to do a blend of those eleven jobs, seven days a week. If you consider that a stay-at-home mum (or dad) might spend fifteen hours a week cleaning at a cost of €10 per hour, this would equate to €150 per week or €7,200 per year. Similarly, to replace twenty hours of child minding a week, at a market value of, say, €15 per hour, would cost over €15,000 a year. This quick price comparison captures at least a flavour of some of the jobs and equivalent costs involved in domestic work, and, amazingly, the total comes in at around €59,000 a year. But before you decide to down tools for better working conditions, allow a drop of some €4,000 to reflect the decrease in labour wages in the last year.

Sometimes I can be quite envious of the declining breed of stay-at-home mums. As I rush to complete the school run before vying with city traffic in the morning, I feel somewhat ostracised by the 'mothers at the school gate brigade' as they saunter and banter at a completely different pace to me. Unfortunately I don't hang around long enough to see if there's any common ground between the species of 'working mum' and 'stay-at-home mum'. I do hope that my lack of interaction doesn't alienate my daughter from those play dates and parties. This is an example of the kind of guilt trip that might fill a working mum's head. Going to work is my safe haven, even with all its challenges. Being a mother is the real challenge for me and, no matter how in control I think I am, I'm always hovering between the familiar and the unknown.

I was introduced to the term 'mumtrepreneur' four years ago when I was asked to be a judge on RTÉ's *Afternoon Show*. The popular TV show had invited viewers to apply to the programme if they had a good business idea or needed help in getting their idea to the next level of development. Mums or recent new mums were their target, in other words mumtrepreneurs. I had only launched WMB a year previously and the 'fit' between my brand and this initiative made perfect sense. Together with two well-seasoned judges, we sifted through the applications, which ranged from the pioneering to the absurd. Our task was to whittle the submissions down to eight in the first instance, then to four and finally to the winning proposal. It was a bit like *Dragon's Den* for mums who were ready to take the leap of faith but without the direct investment. However, they would get media exposure and mentoring, and there was the possibility of financial help. I had little TV experience, but my passion for all things entrepreneurial got me through and I managed to keep my nerves in check. I was inspired by the ability of these talented mums to have a vision and their healthy determination to bring that same vision to fruition. All this was done on the back of rearing children, with little or out-dated business experience. If there was one trait that really surprised me, though, it was their lack of self-belief. This is not a criticism but purely an observation that I make time and time again in my working life. I very much doubt if this would have been the case if we were canvassing men.

On reflection, women tend to be portrayed as being either too confident, bordering on bullish, or too timid, bordering on inept. Confidence issues – whether we have too much or too little – seem to haunt us. If we fight for equality, we're sometimes tagged with the 'burn the bra' brigade or as feisty feminists. As we strive to be individual, we don't necessarily want to be branded as belonging to one particular group. Many of us totally shy away from the 'F' word. We understand the sacrifices that our mothers and grandmothers had to make to ensure we have choice today. We also see the problems and barriers that still exist. But do we actively engage in changing the status quo? I have often seen the lone female rise to prominence and I wonder if she ever considers throwing the ladder back down to the woman behind. I believe there are many women who have fought hard to be successful. They have worked long hours; they have sacrificed so much. But their road has made them hard. They have little interest in making the journey easier for their female colleagues – after all, they struggled, so why should it be any easier for others? Women can be their own worst enemies. Somewhere along the line, when they started mimicking men rather than recognising and celebrating their own unique feminine traits, they lost their identity. They may even have lost their opportunity to be a wife and mother, a best friend or a business confidant. Such was the sacrifice that they felt they had to make; such is the regret some of them must now endure.

My driving force behind *WMB* magazine was to promote women and to connect role models with those in search of inspiration and direction. The brand is much more than a commercial undertaking – it's a calling. My husband often reminds me, and I quote, 'You'll never make any money out of a campaign.' However, WMB Publishing is my way of contributing to the change that needs to take place in our society. Dare I use the words 'equality' and 'change' in the same paragraph without being portrayed as a feminist? Perhaps I am a feminist, though I did not purposely set out to be one. I believe that I have evolved with age, like a good wine. I was always aware of the lack of businesswomen at management level throughout my career. It was only in the last decade that I began to notice a positive change. The media were slow at first to highlight it and seemed almost asleep to the potential and talent that half our population possess. Now they actively go after successful women for their material. I have often been asked by journalists to recommend women for profiling. There are literally thousands of role models just below the radar. I saw a need to propel my vision for change and, in so doing, I have encountered many inequalities on my journey – the pay gap between genders; the absence of women with decision-making powers, both in the political sphere and in company boardrooms; the undervalued role of social entrepreneurship in society – primarily an area which attracts women in their thousands; the total degradation of women worldwide as they are forced into a life of prostitution and kept there by demand. We all need to be a part of the transformation of society's attitude to women and we need strong men behind and beside us. If this makes me a feminist, I will wear the badge willingly, knowing that, like most girl guides, I wear many badges of achievement – not necessarily for big achievements but for my own personal triumphs.

I sometimes get frustrated as I encounter women along the path who are only too happy to ask for help but who give little in return. These are a selfish breed who cannot see beyond their own ambitions, let alone get involved in the agenda for change. For some reason, there are many networks that extol the merits of sisterhood but are as limited in their outlook as the small following that they attract. Women have yet to understand the power of numbers and the benefit of a coherent single message. I say this as a publisher who needs no agenda and one with an insatiable desire to bring change.

Think for a moment what women bring to the table. The fact that women have contributed significantly to our economic growth has given rise to the term 'womenomics'. First coined by *The Economist* back in 2006, womenomics has since been written about in many books and articles.

Fact: Women contribute 40 per cent of the developed World's GDP.

ASPIRING – INDIVIDUAL – VISIONARY – PASSIONATE

In the UK, 80 per cent of consumer goods decisions involve women. Women make up 63 per cent of online shoppers who buy more than once a week. In the next decade or so, women could represent 60 per cent of the UK's personal wealth. In the US, the number of women earning over $100,000 has tripled in the last ten years. At home in Ireland, the number of women in paid employment has more than doubled since the early 1990s. In fact, over 60 per cent of women aged between fifteen and sixty-four years are now in employment, ahead of the EU average.

I have a theory that leaders are not created; they are born. I do, however, wish to make a distinction between leaders who may engage in corporate and political life and those who are entrepreneurs. Between the moment leaders are born and around their seventeenth birthday, their personalities are moulded and their motivators are engaged. Deep inside they have an inner drive which has been lying in wait for the ignition to be switched on. It may take a father, a mother, an inspirational figure or a magical moment for their power to be triggered. Role models play a pivotal part in the lives of our future leaders. Our ancestors had to work long and hard so that we could enjoy a better and more fulfilling existence. They sweated and toiled to build cities and empires. On the other hand, this generation, which has developed such wonderful technologies as the Internet and social media, has somehow managed to destroy the potential of our children's futures in the name of greed. I'm an optimist by nature and I believe that, as with all brick walls, a way over or around this one will be found. We need to re-engage with our inner selves to identify what is now important in our world. I see my daughter with all her wonderful attributes, ignorant of the economic crisis, oblivious of human atrocity, unaware of hatred in the name of religion. I want to bottle up her innocence and manufacture it for the world. At the very least, I want to prepare

122   *Women Mean Business: One Woman's Journey into Entrepreneurship*

her and encourage her to embrace her future as she travels beyond her comfort zone.

Who are our role models in the twenty-first century – those women who have gone beyond the ordinary to achieve the extraordinary? The Forbes brand regularly releases insight lists and their list of 'Most Powerful Women', devised in August 2011, contained few surprises but plenty of diversity. One thing is for sure, the strength of character of these women cannot be questioned:

Number 1:   Angela Merkel – I don't think the Chancellor of Germany needs any introduction, considering she presided over Ireland's financial bailout.

Number 2:   Hillary Clinton – as US secretary of state, this powerful woman has had her fair share of the media's attention.

Number 3:   Dilma Rousseff – the first woman to become president of Latin America's largest economy, Brazil.

Number 4:   Indra Nooyi – she enjoys annual earnings in the millions as PepsiCo's chief executive. Drink it up!

Number 5:   Sheryl Sandberg – this Harvard graduate crossed over from Google to become CEO of Facebook and is all about empowering women.

Number 6:   Melinda Gates – the woman behind the man (Bill Gates) is on a mission to eradicate poverty and bring positive change.

Number 7:   Sonia Gandhi – she is the longest serving president of India's Congress Party.

Number 8:   Michelle Obama – North America's First Lady has been described as Jackie Kennedy with a law degree.

Number 9:   Christine Lagarde – the first woman to head up the International Monetary Fund.

Number 10:   Irene Rosenfeld – the chief executive of Kraft Foods, who wasn't afraid to put it up to Warren Buffet when she bought Cadburys.

So, in a global context these are the women who rule. These are role models who have seen their window of opportunity and jumped right through. They have paved the way for their sisters and daughters who can believe it is possible to make a difference.

Closer to home, we continue to produce our fair share of businesswomen, female entrepreneurs and creative women whose successes span many disciplines. The Managing Director of Microsoft European Operations Centre Cathriona Hallahan is a past winner of the WMB Businesswoman of the Year Awards (2009). Up to recently, Telefónica O2 Ireland was run by Danuta Gray, a respected leader in the highly competitive industry of telecoms. As mentioned, O2 sponsored the WMB Conference & Awards during her reign. Margaret Heffernan, co-owner of the Dunnes Stores chain, is one of Ireland's richest people, having started in the family business at the age of fourteen.

One thing is certain: we are not short of female role models.

Chapter 10

Loving Your Work

*'I've never thought, "I am female so I won't get far."
I just carry on with what I'm doing and see it all as a
wonderful opportunity.'*

**— Damini Kumar, inventor and winner of the Microsoft WMB Woman In
Technology Award 2010**

Month: October
Thought: It's a thin line between love and hate.

I WAS AS GREEN as one of Bill Cullen's penny apples when I launched WMB five years ago, but I was never happier. I used to have to pinch myself in case I was dreaming my new life. And when something particularly good happened, like getting a new sponsor on board or receiving some great feedback, I had to pinch myself pretty hard.

I did have a vision, possibly seen through rose-tinted glasses. I wanted to make a turnover of €1 million and a profit of 10 per cent. I also wanted my own publishing studio, a granite-clad mews that would be feminine and fun, and exude my brand values of aspiring, individual, visionary and passionate. The interior would have to be primarily pink with a hint of blue, with plenty of fresh flowers, thriving plants and wonderful paintings. I wanted a plush pink sofa and bright bean bags for inspirational brainstorming sessions, of which there would be many. Have I painted a clear picture? This is what I wanted then and, although they are cosmetic things for the most part, they are something that I aspire to still.

Imagine a 'Love-Your-Work Barometer' sitting on your desk or hanging around your neck. On a scale of one to ten – where one represents a pretty dismal feeling and ten is nirvana – what number would you score for an average day at work? Do you love your job, your career? How about the people and environment? Is the company culture your culture? Do you skip into work each day or is it more like a drag? Today, I'm hovering at around a seven. I'm coming to the close of another year and I'm here to tell the tale. That's got to be worth a couple of extra points in this environment! Of course, my mind is always blazing ahead at breakneck speed, planning, visualising, theorising. When I eventually catch up with myself and achieve a goal, I have reached the top of my barometer. But I know that it will just re-adjust itself downwards as another goal is set. The 'Infinite Love-Your-Work Barometer' is probably a better name for it!

This begs the question: when did it become so important to love your work as well as your life? Perhaps we set our sights too high. Maybe we've become too self-absorbed. After all, it wasn't so long ago when paid work wasn't an option for married women in Ireland. Our great dilemma now is to juggle an inordinate number of balls at the same time. Eight out of ten times, if I ask a room of people, 'What do you really want in life?' the word 'happiness' comes right back at me. But really, honestly, hand on heart, do you love what you do? Are you happy with your lot? Is working and living the dream all that it's cracked up to be? I will readily admit that I love publishing but there are elements of my work that I would just adore to offload. The author Maria Edgeworth seemed to have called it right when she wrote the words: 'All work and no play makes Jack a dull boy; All play and no work makes Jack a mere toy.' Two centuries later, we still seem to struggle with establishing our work–life balance.

American business author Harvey MacKay wrote: 'Find something you love to do and you'll never have to work a day in your life.' Yes, if you believe in the hype, you can be easily fooled into thinking that you have to love your work. But, seriously, is work not just a means to an end? Do we not tend to look outside of our working day for our fulfilment? Dare to dream and you might soon be disappointed to discover that work is called work because, quite frankly, it is work.

> Definition of 'work', as provided by the *Collins English Dictionary*: 1. Physical or mental effort directed to doing or making something, and 2. Paid employment at a job, trade or profession.

The dictionary definitions of 'work' lack any indication that we should like work, let alone love it. And once the subject of money comes into the equation, work no longer seems like play.

I am asked from time to time to recount my story to groups of women at various events. I am quite selective about what events I speak at, not because I am a prima donna, but because it takes quite a bit of my energy to deliver on the task. Some events have a budget to pay for speakers; others don't. What I've noticed is that, when I get paid, I seem to put more work into the presentation. I'm not saying that I don't prepare for all presentations, but putting a monetary value on a task does make a difference to the way you approach it. Take, for example, hobbies. You might knit for relaxation, but when you're asked to knit something for a paying customer, it suddenly develops into work rather than a labour of love. It somehow becomes too serious to be enjoyable. For women, work needs to be satisfying – it needs to provide passion to some degree. Loving your work is possibly an ultimate goal for most of us. It's a fantastical aim, but it is also a somewhat absurd axiom to suggest that you choose a career path because you love it and, hey presto, you'll love your way through all the hard graft, the roller-coaster ride that is your working life, to come out the other end still loving it. As I think about my career to date, I realise that there have been many signposts along the way – some have led to pastures fair; some have led to near meltdowns. I realise that truly loving most aspects of what I do has helped me to accept those parts that are more challenging.

So, what are the challenging things about work? I have found that getting emotional about it can hold me back. However, I'm not alone. It's funny how women do tend to get emotional about their work. We are always seeking reassurance, confirmation, the comforting pat on the back. As women, we can't seem to separate the professional from the personal. In fact, we probably go out of our way to muddy the waters as we mix the black and white of our work and life into a mild shade of grey. I'd love to be more clinical and detached about work. Certainly, there's always room for improvement when it comes to communication.

Dealing with people – employers, employees, clients, colleagues – can also be a major challenge. Clear communication is vital in a work environment, yet, with the best will in the world, a message can be lost in translation. In some of my previous positions, much of my day was taken up with staff issues. They ranged from listening to unhappy and disgruntled employees to dealing with downright bullies. Perhaps it's the industry I'm in. Media brings its fair share of egos and wannabes. In amongst them you'll find a pool of creative, talented individuals who sometimes need to be cultivated and given a chance to shine.

Human resources issues are big business these days as employees' rights seem to take precedence over those of the employer. I grew up believing that if you weren't getting on well in your job or with your employer, you just left. If you genuinely felt unhappy, your time was up. I can't understand why someone would waste his or her precious life working for a company or employer that he or she doesn't respect. I also think that, like with relationships, you have to work in many jobs before you find the right one for you. 'But what if there are no jobs?' I hear you ask. There are always jobs and opportunities for those willing to work hard and go that extra mile. Yes, it may take a while and it may be a struggle, but believe in your ability and someone else will recognise your potential. Tip: if you lose your job, or are down on your luck, be prepared to do anything to keep yourself occupied. I have made pizzas at 6.00 a.m. in the morning (from scratch); I have collected foreign exchange students at the airport at midnight. I will always do whatever it takes to make things work, to pay the bills, to provide for my family. I have often seen people who are too proud or too much in denial. They would rather hide away than 'lower their standards'. I have huge admiration for someone who will muck in, at anything. It is this person who will shine in the long run.

I came across some interesting research recently on the very topic of the career perspectives of women and men. We promoted the findings in issue 27 of *WMB* (p. 39):

Accenture is an international management consultancy and has supported our annual Awards since launch. They are one of the few blue chip companies who celebrate International Women's Day each year in Ireland on a large scale and have some superb diversity initiatives to include in their Accent on Women Programme. The global research which they completed recently was entitled 'Reinvent Opportunity: Looking Through a New Lens' and involved surveying more than 3,400 professionals across 29 countries, with equal responses from both women and men. Fewer than half of all respondents were satisfied with their current jobs, but nearly three-quarters planned to stay with their current employers. Why such dissatisfaction? Reasons included: being underpaid; lack of opportunity for growth; no opportunity for career advancement; and, lastly, feeling trapped. Despite these issues, more than half of respondents were looking to develop their knowledge and/or skills set to achieve their career objectives and within their current employ. Women were somewhat less likely than men to say they had asked for a pay rise (44% v. 48%), and promotion (28% v. 39%). While more than half of respondents (55% of women and 57% of men) were satisfied with the career levels they had reached, more women reported that their careers were not 'fast tracked'. When asked about factors that help women advance in their organisations, more than two-thirds of women (68%) but only about half of men (55%) cited hard work and long hours. Less than one-third of respondents from both groups reported that they had a formal or informal mentor. It is this point that resonates with me as a female entrepreneur. I believe that successful entrepreneurs should go out of their way to pass on their experiences (good and bad!). There was also an interesting 'generational difference' in that, whilst all groups cited higher pay as the top reason for pursuing career advancement, the youngest respondents – Generation Y (those born after 1979) – were significantly more motivated by pay than Generation X (those born between 1965 and 1978) or Baby Boomers (those born before 1964).

So money is a motivator, and more so for the current generation of job seekers. Considering the gender pay gap is alive and kicking, as women we have some road to travel to reach parity with our male colleagues. It makes loving your work that bit harder for us, I guess. However, it has been my experience that women don't ask for pay increases or promotion as readily as men. This point is borne through in the survey's results. For some reason, we seem to think that employers (of which I am one) will volunteer an increase and this is rarely the case. In an environment where there is an oversupply of human talent against a short supply of jobs, it is even less likely that there will be an offer of any kind coming your way. And if we are going to take the bull by the horns and put a value on our heads, we need to be far more strategic in our approach and far less emotional.

I've put together some suggestions, which you should consider before you go into the lion's lair looking for more loot. They're backed up by years of experience in negotiation on both sides of the fence – that of employee and of employer.

- Put yourself in your employer's shoes. Look at how the company is performing overall. Although your department may be meeting targets, the company could be haemorrhaging elsewhere. A company in the red is looking to cut to the bone, not add to the fat.
- Research trends within your industry to find out if there is much mobility.
- Review your own performance. Can you put a monetary value on a recent project or initiative which you have successfully completed and can take ownership of? Is this a one-off or of sustainable benefit to the company?
- Identify the motives behind wanting your increase or promotion. Is it for recognition of your hard work? Is it to meet increased personal financial commitments? Is it to put you 'on par' with your colleagues?
- If you are unsuccessful in your endeavours, what is your next move? Rejection can be a bitter pill to swallow and there's nothing worse than a disgruntled employee, especially if it's you!
- Have a Plan B. If you don't get exactly what you want, is there another way to achieve your desired objective. Perhaps consider a phased approach to promotion. Suggest goals to work to which add real benefit to the company and will guarantee you your increase within an agreed time frame. If money is out of the question, is job flexibility an option, or perhaps an increase in your annual leave or other benefits?

Believe it or not, employers want solutions to issues. But also be wary as they might be looking to trim the fat further. You just need to box clever and prepare. I have come across so many different personalities, so many good and not-so-good individuals. Positivity and a proactive approach are two of the key traits for me when working with others. There's nothing worse than a moan. Moaners rarely succeed in life and feel they are owed a living. They seldom come up with insightful suggestions and would fall into the 'clock watching' brigade. They sap your energy with their negativity and, although they may survive in a larger organisation, they are dead weight in a small set-up. Passion is also a trait that I'm attracted to. I have it in abundance and it can be contagious.

However, as a business owner, there is a limit to what you can expect from your staff, especially in a tight economic setting. I have learned that no one is indispensable. If you feel someone is going to jump ship and you have genuinely done everything in your power to retain their talent, you need to let them go. You will lose that person's experience and there may be more pressure on you for a time, but eventually you will find another candidate who will do the job equally well, if not better. New blood can bring new thinking. Learn to accept that change is inevitable and can bring great things. There are a couple of people I have worked with who I wish I could have retained. Sometimes people leave their job because they are unhappy about money or benefits, but it can be as much about growth and advancement as anything monetary. I have purposely kept the WMB team small. I fortunately work in an industry that thrives on flexibility. Writers, designers, photographers – they all now tend to work freelance. I don't have the overheads of large publishing houses but I can still produce top-quality work from a panel of contributors. The recession has brought many challenges and I haven't been able to advance in finding my complete dream team. However, I remain on the look out and will let fate intervene when the time is right.

Staffing aside, the other 'S' that challenges my almost-perfect job is sales. There are so many aspects to sales. I totally acknowledge that you are your brand and everything you do, right down to your compliment slips, should reflect your brand values. You are constantly selling yourself and your wares. When you're passionate about a product or service and you put thought into the 'fit' between your brand and other people's brands, it can be a match made in heaven. I purposely only contact those companies with whom there is a natural fit. I need a high conversion rate when selling sponsorship or a unique offering as my time is precious. My potential client's time is even more so. If you believe in the fit, research your target and respect their time, you will succeed. If you go into something in a half-hearted way, with little thought and even less preparation, expect to fail. Once the recession hit, advertising became a dirty word. At the best of times, it can be difficult to convince clients to part with their hard-earned cash or, as Dragon Duncan Bannatyne would say, part with his children's inheritance.

I sometimes hit a brick wall when selling. No one wants to talk to me and I begin to feel like the embodiment of 'junk' mail. However, once I realise that it's not personal, I take a step back, do something else and return to fight another day. It's all about perseverance without reaching panic point. If I had a magic wand I would conjure up a clone of me. In the meantime, I have to work twice as hard to deliver my targets. I can also get tied up in knots internally if I bite off more than I can chew. But you always live on the edge as an entrepreneur – just beyond your comfort zone. At times like this, I tend to listen to my husband when he says: 'What's the worst that can happen?' I review the situation, acknowledge all that's right about it and work on fixing what's wrong. In other words, I put the task, project or goal into perspective.

I guess I find selling, especially advertising, frustrating. As the recession steamed in, less and less people were willing to talk to me and many of those who did were really only paying lip service. Overnight, there was a paralysis of power and decision making.

Advertising spends froze and the message was not delivered coherently to vested parties. Just think of the number of times you have sent someone a proposal and received nothing back. You follow up once, maybe twice, and still nothing. Your proposal may be your priority but nine times out of ten it's not a priority for your client. I wish more people would learn to say no gracefully and quickly rather than say nothing. Irish people are the worst. It's as though we don't want to offend. But we do offend when we don't acknowledge. I'll accept a 'yes' gladly, I'll be disappointed by a 'no' – but please don't remain silent and leave me guessing.

I make it my business to respond to all queries. I guess this is because I know how difficult it can be to put yourself out there. I wasn't born to sell. I may be good at it and it comes naturally in certain contexts, but it's not my chosen profession. I love being creatively commercial, which brings in the whole sales thing. But cold calls, phone sales, door-to-door sales – cringe! So, when someone is trying to sell me something, I do listen. I don't waste time but I am polite and I'm decisive.

The last aspect of my job that can sometimes drive me into a near meltdown is money. To clarify, I love making money. I love having a positive bottom line and I certainly like spending money. I am a confirmed shopaholic and wouldn't expect anyone else to feed this expensive habit of mine. If you do the crime, you do the time, and I'm a serial offender when it comes to using my credit cards. But there's nothing more wonderful than rewarding yourself for a job well done. It doesn't happen often in the current climate, but it's important to recognise your achievements and what better way than with a spending spree. To deny yourself is just too cruel. Projecting cash flows is vital for your company's survival and I do this task with quite a degree of accuracy. During the times that overdrafts are maxed, and your debtors are slow to pay, money suddenly takes over your life. I tend to go into detox mode at the mere notion of running out of money. A decade ago, debtor days could run to seventy-five days in publishing. This improved vastly when there was plenty of cash around. Now everyone is complaining about the gap between providing a service and getting paid for it. Know your clients, build a relationship with them, give them a first-class service and they will pay you within an acceptable time frame, no matter what the climate. However, never take your eye off the money ball. In five years I've only had one bad debt. It was with a well-known franchise business at the time and, although they acknowledged the debt, I never saw the cash. I just heard a lot of excuses. Yes, I could have gone legal and, yes, I would have won, but I balanced my time and put extra systems in place to ensure that it didn't happen again. There's no foolproof system, but dealing with credible clients is one of this gal's ten commandments. And, while I'm on the subject, here are my commandments in full:

WMB's Ten Commandments

1. Know your cash flows; expect the unexpected.
2. Only do business with blue chip clients. Better to be paid than to be stung.
3. Surround yourself with positivity.
4. Go out of your comfort zone, often.
5. Learn something new.
6. When you lose, don't lose the lesson.
7. Throw down the ladder – women should support one another.
8. Open your arms to change, but don't let go of your values.
9. Avoid procrastination.
10. Believe.

Magazine publishing is a passion and I can't think of anything else that I'd rather do. Actually, strike that. Writing books could come a close second. I always knew there was at least one book in me. Imagine actually getting paid to sit down and dream up a whole series. I do tend to throw myself into the project at hand.

I've always done so. When I worked in radio, I wanted to be a production assistant, script writer and presenter, all rolled into one. I still think I could be all these things, but for now I need to see my current passion develop into a thriving success. I had thought when I was studying for my Diploma in Applied Finance that I could be an accountant. Gosh, talk about hopping from right brain to left brain overnight! Fortunately, the idea didn't stick – accountants make me come out in hives.

There's always going to be aspects of your career and life that you'd like to change or would even like to forget. Stepping up to the plate is what separates followers from leaders. There are three types of people in life – those who think about it; those who talk about it; and those who do something about it. Which one are you?

Chapter 11

Is the Price Right?

'The only person that can stop you from doing what you want is yourself.'

– Lucy Gaffney, chairman of Communicorp; interviewed in WMB, issue 17

Month: November
Thought: Avoid procrastination.

HAVE YOU EVER visited New York? If you have, you'll be familiar with street traders, one-man bands, who sell trinkets, coffee, hot dogs, whatever. They have a smile on their faces and fire in their bellies. They are sole traders who turn a buck, which is well earned, and they don't intimidate. My point is that there are always alternatives if someone is willing to explore them.

I get really frustrated when I see people begging in our streets. For starters, I don't know who to help and who to avoid, although I can say, quite categorically, that I would never help someone sitting below a cash-dispensing machine. Begging is big business and it's tax free. It's an acceptable practice for some cultures, but it contributes nothing back to our society and deters visitors to our cities and custom to our shops. So, why should it be tolerated in our streets? If I have to close my business in the morning, I'm entitled to nothing – I can't claim unemployment benefit like most other individuals – and this is despite having contributed over two decades of stamps. In some ways, because there is no fail-safe position, it makes me even more determined to succeed. So, excuse me when I get a bit hot under the collar about our 'begging for a living' street urchins who are dropped to prime locations for the morning rush and picked up afterwards.

I would imagine that one of the greatest deterrents for those setting up in business today is the possibility of failure. These would-be entrepreneurs, if they failed, wouldn't be able to claim any benefits. While a single person may be in a position to take this risk, it's very different if you have dependants.

I wasn't brave enough in my former permanent, pensionable, well-paid and single-status position to take the leap. More correctly, the time wasn't right, partly because I really loved my job and partly because I had just built a house and had a nice hefty mortgage. But then everything changed: I met my future husband, had my lightbulb moment, the dynamics of my position altered and it was my time.

So, you want to be an entrepreneur; you want to stand on your own two feet; you want to build your empire. If it were easy, everyone would be doing it. If failure didn't exist, there would be little point in trying. Let's take a look at the figures. I'm a firm believer in trends and what happens in the US tends to follow through in the UK, and eventually in Ireland. Figures released under the Kauffman Index of Entrepreneurial Activity (US) shows that, last year, 565,000 new businesses were started per month by new and repeat entrepreneurs. The 340 out of every 100,000 adults who started businesses each month during 2010 represented a 4 per cent increase over 2008 figures. Overall, men are substantially more likely to start businesses each month than women and it transpires that an aging population has led to a rising share of new entrepreneurs in the 55 to 64 age group, representing 22.9 per cent of new entrepreneurs in 2010 (as opposed to 14.5 per cent back in 1996). Kauffman's Index shows the highest start-up rate in the last fifteen years against a backdrop of the Great Recession. It does beg the question as to what motivates someone to launch during a period such as this. This might be as much down to lack of choice (a necessity motive) as to the desire to be their own boss (an opportunity motive). However, the research highlighted a worrying trend in jobless entrepreneurship – the preference for self-employed individuals to remain in one-man or one-woman shows rather than take on employees. If this is the case, the idea of promoting entrepreneurship as a means to resolving our unemployment crisis in Ireland might well be misplaced.

There's a whole new movement afoot to encourage young people to consider entrepreneurship as a career option. When you're young you just go for it because you've no inhibitions, only dreams. Or at least that's how it should be. I do worry when I look at the teenagers around me. Their desire to stretch themselves isn't that apparent as they seek the easy option, time and time again. I know that, although I wasn't a whizz kid in school, I was always scribbling, always doodling. I even wrote a poetry book by the time I was sixteen, which now gathers dust in the attic. I played the guitar, visited the art gallery frequently, dreamed up all sorts of magical stories. I regularly babysat and got a holiday job, which provided me with a sense of achievement and a small taste of independence. Today, our teenagers are not as hungry. As they immerse themselves in *Keeping Up with the Kardashians*, *Sweet Sixteen* and Jedward's latest antics, it's hard for them to come back down to reality – any reality. Twitter is the new talk, and the gossip on Bieber, Gaga and Hilton is neverending. They can rehearse all the lines from Justin Bieber's 'Never Say Never', but don't ask them to recite anything from *Hamlet*. Theirs is a world of fame, fashion and photo opportunities. I'm all for having aspirations, but it won't be long before the rags-to-riches stories implode to be replaced by the important lesson that only through hard work will rewards come.

The cynic in me tells me that our Government is driving this entrepreneurship initiative so that the next generation will be responsible for themselves – after all, there'll be little or no state pension when their time is up. Entrepreneurship is an opportunity for our country, but it needs to be supported. Mentoring is great, but money is far more meaningful. Our current, well-seasoned entrepreneurs are dropping away by the hundreds, such is the strangle hold on cash by the banks. Realistically, how can we encourage entrepreneurship if the basic ingredient of start-up capital and/or working capital is non-existent? Female entrepreneurship is even more challenging. We tend to work in the service sector, which receives little funding and even less recognition of its vital contribution to our economy. We already know that we start up companies at a much lower rate than our male counterparts. Technology and the sciences are the future – sectors that are primarily male dominated. But wait, don't women account for over 60 per cent of all EU graduates? Perhaps we're studying the wrong subjects. In a bid to encourage female role models, last year WMB linked up with Microsoft to create the Woman in Technology Award. I soon discovered that, for such a small country, we have a fantastic pool of talented individuals working and leading in this sector. I hope that, through this new initiative, we are encouraging in some small way more women to step up and be counted in technology.

Once again, the US appears to have its finger on the pulse when it comes to hard figures on female entrepreneurship. *The American Express OPEN State of Women-Owned Businesses Report* details trends in the area of female entrepreneurship and its value to the US economy. The information, which is taken from last year's US Census Bureau data, indicates that women start businesses at 1.5 times the national rate, and now own an estimated 8.1 million enterprises, which generate nearly $1.3 trillion in revenues and employ 7.7 million Americans.

The Report paints a picture of growth in female entrepreneurship over the last fourteen years. Its findings depend on whether you look at trends within the population of women-owned firms over time, how women-owned companies have performed compared to their male counterparts or how they are faring compared to the economy as a whole. Within the population of women-owned firms, you can see a steady growth but a lack of progress up the size continuum. When comparing like with like, small and mid-size women-owned firms are keeping pace with the national average – and are topping the very sluggish growth seen among men-owned firms in the 1997–2011 period. However, something is putting women-owned firms off their stride as they grow larger; within the entrepreneurial marathon, they fall behind when they enter the 100-employee-plus and million-dollar 'anchor leg' of the race.

The *GEM (Global Entrepreneurship Monitor) Ireland 2008 National Report* showed that Ireland is, at heart, an entrepreneurial nation, with a rate of early-stage entrepreneurial activity at 7.6 per cent and established entrepreneurs at 9 per cent of the adult population. At the time, this represented an average of 2,800 people setting up businesses every month. The GEM report noted that, in more challenging times, there is an increase in the numbers turning to entrepreneurship as a means of creating employment for themselves. One in four (27 per cent) of early-stage entrepreneurs were serial entrepreneurs, i.e. they had already been involved in previous set-ups. The rate of early-stage entrepreneurial activity among men stands at 9.5 per cent (2010), whereas the rate for women is at 3.9 per cent. This implies that men are twice as likely as women to set up their own business.

Last year (2010), the GEM report revisited Ireland's spirit for business and found that 56 per cent of early-stage entrepreneurs admitted it was harder to start a business in 2010 compared to the previous year, with our entrepreneurs citing, in almost equal proportions, necessity and opportunity motives for going out on their own. Perceived opportunities to start a business declined by about 50 per cent from 2007 to 2010. The fear-of-failure rate remained comparatively high compared to other countries surveyed. However, the most striking indicator is the staggering growth in the percentage of necessity-motivated early-stage entrepreneurs from 2007 to 2010. All this implies that such people were not hopeful about their entrepreneurial potential before the recession and were possibly more likely to stay in paid employment, rather than start businesses with opportunity motives. Yet, with fewer job opportunities during these challenging times, some people needed entrepreneurship to provide a livelihood.

This brings me to the question – are entrepreneurs born or manufactured? I asked this question recently to one of Ireland's successful businesswomen, Sarah Newman, who has had her fair share of good and not-so-good publicity. Both her parents were entrepreneurs who experienced bouts of good and bad fortune, so why did she follow such a precarious path? For Sarah, it seemed to be a combination of necessity (she had two small children to support) and opportunity (she firmly believed in her business model which took her on a journey from zero to hero in a decade). In my case, I seemed to turn my back on career success as I wanted to follow my vision and, most importantly, I wanted to build on it. I often wonder if I knew back then what I know now, would I do it all over again? My answer is a resounding 'Yes.' I do ponder what motivates people to set up businesses, to start from scratch, to be inventors. It must be so much easier to run a family business. You're born into the role; it's in your blood. You don't have to interview for the job and you have the trust and support of your parents and siblings. You have insider knowledge from the off. But setting up something totally new and innovative brings a greater degree of risk as you cross the sands of uncertainty, with no steps to follow and only your footprints behind. I think a better question to ask is: what traits are most common in successful entrepreneurs? The answer? Resilience, vision, positivity, self-belief. And are these traits hard-wired into our DNA or acquired over time? I believe both to be true. There are many individuals born into poverty who turn their hardship into a catalyst to succeed. Equally, there are those born into privileged positions who lack lustre and will never have the attributes necessary to achieve. Your surrounds will influence you, role models will define you, and your heart will guide you.

As mentioned, one of the main deterrents for those wishing to take the plunge is the fear of failure. Think of the giant American energy, commodities and services company Enron. People tend to ignore the fact that, at its height, it employed some 22,000 staff with revenues in excess of $100 billion . People do, however, remember the scandal, corruption and eventual closure of the company in 2001. Closer to home, there was the company DeLorean, manufacturers of the DMC-12 sports car that many of us would recognise as the 'Back to the Future car' with its gull-wing doors and sleek finish. It opened its factory in Dunmurry, Northern Ireland, despite the fact that a report to one of its investors had given it a 90 per cent possibility of failure (or a one-in-ten chance of success). DeLorean went bankrupt in late 1982. More recently, in 2009, the high-street retail chain Woolworths, which was better known as 'Woolies', went into administration, resulting in the loss of around 27,000 jobs. These are examples of three very different industries, all well-known brands, all leaving the bitter taste of failure behind.

There are plenty of figures bandied about on the success and failure of new entities. Out of every 1,000 new businesses, 40 per cent fail within the first year (this is more likely to be 90 per cent in my sector) and 80 per cent within five years. But, even after five years up and running, you're still not safe: 80 per cent of those who reach their fifth birthday fail before they ring in a new decade. Have I turned you off the idea of 'living the dream' yet?

In Ireland, we tend to look with distain on failure, whereas our American friends embrace those failures as experiences that create the sound foundations of future successes. It was Thomas Edison who said: 'Many of life's failures are men who did not realise how close they were to success when they gave up.' Edison had worked out no fewer than 3,000 theories about light bulbs before he succeeded. He rightly acknowledged that 'Genius is one per cent inspiration and 99 per cent perspiration.' And it was the father of modern physics, Einstein, who said, 'We can't solve problems by using the same kind of thinking we used when we created them.' The common bond that links inventors, entrepreneurs and visionaries is their 'emotional resilience'.

Take Walt Disney, whose mantra 'If you can dream it, you can do it', mentioned earlier in this book, is embedded in my psyche. Having created the character of Oswald the Lucky Rabbit, Disney learned the hard way that he did not hold ownership of the character, and that most of his artists had committed themselves to working for the distributor instead. His company was literally taken from under him, with the exception of one artist Ub Lwerks, who remained loyal. It was this artist who assisted Walt in creating his most famous of characters – Mickey Mouse – in the early 1920s. Another setback (or failure) occurred when Disney tried to distribute Mickey Mouse to MGM Studios who told him the idea of a giant mouse would never work – it would simply terrify women! This and many other stories show that we shouldn't fear failure, but we should embrace the lessons learned from it. Otherwise, we wouldn't have the joys of electricity, motion pictures, cartoons, television, computers, flight and, my favourite, the vacuum cleaner! These wonderful inventions, which we can sometimes take for granted, were discovered on the back of sleepless nights, frustration, near penury and, dare I say it, failure.

I have thought of failure on a number of occasions over the past five years. Initially, in the first year or so of WMB, it was my pride that I was worried about, but as my business progressed there was more at stake. I wasn't prepared to fail and quickly banished bouts of doubt with a more determined focus on the prize, which, by the way, wasn't money, although earning a decent wage would have been welcomed. I had launched a brand that was all about women and included a publication with the objective of profiling successful role models and business mentors. I didn't want to fail in my goal to inspire other women to succeed. I wanted my publication, as the only dedicated read for business-women, to succeed. *WMB* is not about fashion and frills; it is a channel for stories of success and failure and learning.

I believe, as I work through my moments of panic, sleepless nights, near disasters and countless disappointments, that I am building momentum. I have huge energy and enthusiasm about the WMB brand. When I come in contact with those who 'get it', the feeling I get is as electric as any of Edison's lightbulbs. I have created a first, something original, and I need to maintain my emotional resilience in order to get people to follow. And all of this I am doing on the back of one of the worst recessions the world has ever experienced. Seriously, have I put you off yet?

When I think of failure, I think that it is short-lived. We all have, at some stage of our lives, tasted failure. It may have been in an exam, in sports, in an interview, in a relationship, in a sales pitch. I do think that the word 'failure' might be too strong in most instances; 'disappointment' might be more suitable. It doesn't necessarily follow that success always comes with hard work.

However, little work brings far less chance of success and, indeed, less chance of the feeling of self-worth. I've experienced more satisfaction on completing a hard project than an easier one. I seem to have an internal gage that measures success by my own terms – and I am a tough taskmaster when it comes to self-achievement.

So, if it is a fact that failure is far more frequent than success in the world of enterprise; if it is far more likely that you will be paying yourself an intern's wage than a bank manager's bonus; if it is highly conceivable that you will be working 24/7 rather than 9.00 a.m. to 5.00 p.m., why on earth would you dip your toe into this ocean of uncertainty? The answer is in one little word that holds an infinite amount of possibilities – belief. Such is your belief in an invention, a product, a service, a brand that your belief is what eventually separates you from millions of others. Yes, your resilience will be tested, and often. Yes, you will experience plenty of self-doubt. But it's a positive thing to doubt yourself sometimes. It is through doubt that you ask yourself probing questions, allowing you to discard those rose-tinted glasses and acquire a clearer vision of your path ahead.

I have always stood firm that setting your goals and committing them to paper will take you quite a distance on your journey to success. One of the necessary evils of entrepreneurship is to focus on the financial side of things, sometimes to the detriment of your vision. This lack of strategy is more prevalent in an environment where business is hard to come by and even harder to get compensated for. So, let's have two sets of goals. First, the 'must reach' items, like a lean working environment with tight controls on cash and firm financial goalposts. And, second, the aspirational items, for instance, I want to take the summer off so that I can enjoy watching my children grow up; or I want to commit to further education; or I want to identify a new business opportunity that will grow the brand. All too often of late, I have seen how the bottom line has taken over as the creative takes a back step in businesses, and all in the name of survival. So, apart from belief, you also need a fair share of patience with an even larger degree of determination.

The following list describes the main risks of entrepreneurship, according to my experience.

The Real Risks and Trade-offs of Setting Up Your Own Business

* *Time* – this is one of your most valuable commodities. You will learn to think smarter and value what little time you have for leisure and your loved ones.
* *Money* – expect to pay yourself a pittance for at least three to five years. Yes, you can have a fantastic business plan with a nice salary detailed, but when push comes to shove your remuneration will fall way behind other overheads.
* *Security* – it is one of the most naked moments of your working life when you leave as an employee to launch into entrepreneurship. Becoming an entrepreneur is like bungee jumping without the elastic cord.
* *Pension* – you know you want one; you know you need one. You may already have one from your previous life. However, pensions are one of many perceived luxuries that get bumped to the bottom of the list. There's one certainty if you don't have a pension – your later years won't be all that golden.
* *Fear of failure* – like a hangover, the fear comes, plays havoc with your head and leaves you feeling exhausted. Avoid at all costs.
* *Lost identity* – entrepreneurs live the dream 24/7 which means that you are likely to become a total bore about your business. For the sake of your relationship, ensure your partner is totally on-board and laid back to boot.
* *Personality switch* – unlike identity loss, you will go through phases of personality switch. This is where you are expected (or even forced) to take on the persona of Cinderella when at home (all scrubbing and cleaning with a 'no show' from your fairy godmother); editor- in-chief Miranda Priestly in *The Devil Wears Prada* (all hiss and no humility in the office when things go

wrong); and Glenn Close in *Fatal Attraction* (you know you've no interest in having an affair but you still want to boil that rabbit!). Yes, you have to be all things to a lot of people as you multitask. Once you're aware of possible negative outcomes, think more along the lines of Meg Ryan in *When Harry Met Sally* – fake it and you'll sail right through!

- *The myth of the finish line* – what finish line? As you start to invest sweat and tears into your business, you do so with the false belief that there is an end to your journey. Indeed, you believe that your pot of gold will appear way before your grey hair as you meticulously plan your exit strategy. Don't be fooled as, once you start your journey, endless challenges and opportunities will present and the finish line will become a small dot on the very distant horizon. Let's face it: retirement is for bankers, politicians and lottery winners.

The Rewards for this Female Entrepreneur

Founder of The Body Shop Anita Roddick spelled out her motivation as an entrepreneur when she said: 'I have always found that my view of success has been iconoclastic: success to me is not about money or status or fame; it's about finding a livelihood that brings me joy and self-sufficiency and a sense of contributing to the world' (www.anitaroddick.com). Roddick's business model followed the triple bottom line philosophy – people, planet and profit. Although her subsequent sale of The Body Shop to giant cosmetic firm L'Oreal had a mixed reaction, one thing is certain – she made her mark. These are some of the rewards for entrepreneurs that I take from my own experience:

- *Recognition* – this is one of the motivational driving forces for entrepreneurs. Since the age of sixteen, I have always believed that I would make a difference, leave my imprint in some way. I have some ideas of how I can achieve my goal and it will take time and plenty of hard work. Perhaps through the WMB

Awards I have already helped make a difference in highlighting the fantastic work that women do in an economic and social context.

- *Options* – I like to make my own decisions and will stand or fall on the choices I make. It is so important to be able to act on opportunity, to be able to control your own destiny, to sink or swim on your own merits. Entrepreneurship gives you choice without the red tape.

- *The two 'Cs'* – being able to use my commerciality and creativity. Unfortunately you tend to get 'pegged' or 'boxed in' when working in an organisation. As an owner/manager, however, you have the opportunity to feed your creative cravings as well as deliver on your commercial instincts.

- *Flexibility* – 'homepreneur' is the new buzz word as more and more people opt out of commuting, paying unnecessary office rentals and other overheads. As a business owner, your industry sector will very much dictate your location. I like physically going out to work, possibly because I have limited office space at home. However, I enjoy a lot of flexibility, which has been greatly helped by the advancement of technology. Flexibility cannot be under-estimated. The idea that I can go to my daughter's school play and, in the same day, work though my correspondence on the move, or even take a meeting or two, ensures I am both produc-tive and highly motivated.

- *Unlimited potential* – there are no barriers or boundaries as an entrepreneur, just bountiful opportunities. If money is your motive, become a millionaire; if people come before profit, intro-duce a social or charitable dimension to your business.

- *Ownership and relationships* – as an entrepreneur, you have an opportunity to lead rather than follow. You have a capacity to build and expand rather than just 'exist'. Although you don't tend to turn away business as a new start-up, once you become more established you can pick and choose your business partners. These partners will most likely share your company ethos and values. Relationships built on honesty survive and thrive.

- *Family* – the most important aspect of my life. As an entrepreneur, you have a sense of purpose. For a successful entrepreneur it must be so fulfilling to know that you can provide for your family. You can be a role model for your children and encourage them to become independent, confident young adults. You can ensure you have a certain quality of comfort and lifestyle.

Finally, and I think most importantly, you can be true to yourself. As a result, you are a happier and more fulfilled individual with an ability to share your life experiences in a positive way. I know I'm not there yet, but I compare my journey to baking a cake – I have all the ingredients and I just need to ensure that I get the mix and timing exactly right.

Chapter 12

Time for Change

*'Entrepreneurship drives society, not just the economy...
If entrepreneurship drives the wealth which drives the
economy it ultimately drives society. It's the beginning
of the domino effect.'*

**– Julie Meyer, founder of Ariadne Capital and Entrepreneur Country;
interviewed in *WMB*, issue 23**

Month: December
Thought: Open your arms to change, but don't let go of your values.

IT HAS BEEN FIVE YEARS since I launched WMB Publishing
and I've learned some hard lessons. The most difficult was
possibly the realisation that I had to start over, almost from
scratch, as the recession eroded my valuable working relationships. For me, that's what business is all about – relationships. It
takes time to cultivate a good working relationship, which should
be built on trust, respect and mutual opportunity. But what's a
gal to do when half her clients disappear over night? Well, survive
of course! On realising that many of my contacts had been made
redundant while many others lost their power to spend, I had to
re-evaluate my offering. For instance, my advertising rate card for

the magazine had to be totally revised – down. Finding sponsorship was more difficult as some clients used the recession as an opt-out clause and others as a bargaining tool. A fair deal was harder to strike and I had to look at bringing added value to any new deal that was done. However, this value has to be carefully measured – sometimes, the reward mightn't justify the effort.

Fortunately, there was a core of business people who maintained their fit with the brand and, in time, I rebuilt any lost business through new revenue streams and opportunities. Nothing was out of the question. I constantly thought of how my brand could be extended, of how my time could be best utilised. I revised my goals and eradicated 'time stealers'. As a result, I thought smarter and viewed the opportunity cost of each of my decisions. When taking on a new piece of work, I broadly looked at four aspects: the time it would take to complete; the risk and reward; the benefit to the brand; and whether it was of sustainable benefit or a one-off. I remained resilient throughout and it is this attribute that has helped pave the way for me through survival and towards success. I continue to surround myself with like-minded individuals – those who are not afraid of hard work; those who share similar values; those who are born survivors.

It's unnerving as you watch great people and brands fold. I've little sympathy for the banks and builders in this recession, but I have huge compassion for those entrepreneurs and businesspeople who simply couldn't move quickly enough in order to survive. Many of my colleagues working in corporate Ireland and working for themselves have acknowledged the huge shift from growth to decline, the change in dialogue from the positive to the negative. I firmly believe that those start-ups and more established companies who continue to ride the economic storm will come out the other end as leaner, more competitive models with lots of promise. The Celtic tiger economy provided some great opportunities that we tend to forget. It awakened an entrepreneurial spirit which I believe will guarantee our futures. As with any recession, there are opportunities. The smaller business can move more quickly. We can establish low-cost enterprises in a matter of months, not years. Now, I'm not suggesting for a moment that we should ditch the planning process – look where lack of planning and lack of controls got us thus far. However, if we could spread around the 'can do' attitude, then the power of people will get things moving again. Entrepreneurs provide employment and those important returns for the Exchequer. We create community spirit and tend to better our local environment as well as making a difference in the wider economic context.

Entrepreneurs have vision – that's our unique selling point. The difficulty is that there is little or no cash available to start a business. Although female entrepreneurs tend to use their own capital or very little capital, their progress can be slow. The trick is to find an opportunity that involves little start-up capital – an idea that requires your mental sense rather than physical cents! The Internet arena has allowed for an explosion of possibilities. Technology has changed how we communicate with each other and it has opened up a world of options for stay-at-home mums who may want to engage in commerce. It has allowed small businesses to keep costs tight, and it allows for flexibility and working remotely. It has allowed this gal to engage with designers and illustrators based thousands of miles away; it has enabled me to work with some great writers and journalists to our mutual benefit; it has given me a better balance, although I readily admit I don't seek perfect equilibrium. It has allowed me write this book with my daughter's playful voice and my husband's supportive tone in the background.

What lessons can we learn from past mistakes? One thing is certain – if women were more involved in the decision-making process of governments, financial institutions and corporations, our economic landscape would be very different now. The age of testosterone-fuelled decision making is ending as women's attributes – flexibility, resilience and reliability – come out tops in this climate that demands adaptability to change. The last decade has seen a huge role revolution for women. Some might argue that by gaining our financial independence we have forgotten our family values. Others would argue that women who 'want it all' are only working themselves into early graves.

One of the world's leading global management consulting firms McKinsey & Company has produced some great research on the whole area of women and their potential contribution to our economic growth and, now, to our recovery. In 2007, McKinsey published *Women Matter: Gender diversity, a corporate performance driver*. This report demonstrated a link between a company's performance and the proportion of women serving on its governing body. In *Women Matter 2*, published in 2008, McKinsey identified the reasons for this performance effect by examining the leadership styles that women leaders typically adopt. In 2009, they conducted a survey of about 800 business leaders worldwide which confirmed that certain leadership behaviours typically adopted by women are critical to good business performance in this post-crisis world. In 2010, *Women Matter* confirmed that women were still under-represented on boards of corporations, although improvements have been seen in this area in some countries. However, gender diversity within executive committees remained very low. And yet gender diversity in the top management of corporations remains a hot topic: three years after the first *Women Matter* study, the link between the presence of women on executive committees and better financial performance is still valid. This most recent McKinsey study revealed that a majority of leaders, both men and women, now recognise gender diversity as a performance driver, while also showing that actual implementation of gender-diversity measures in corporations remains limited. This is not surprising as the achievement of gender diversity is not at the top of – nor even on – companies' strategic agendas. The study identified those measures that tend to be more effective in increasing female representation, high-lighting in particular the impact of CEO commitment and women's individual development programmes.

Women are ideally suited to the new leadership style that has been widely embraced of late. The old style was top-down, and based on command and control. The new approach, often called an influence model of leadership, is better suited to women. It is time for change. As frustration leads to freeze, it's up to each one of us to roll up our sleeves. We need to rebuild our futures with firm ground rules so that our sons and daughters will not spend their lifetime paying for our past mistakes. (I use the word 'our', as we voted our decision-making baboons into power in the first place!)

I often wonder who is best positioned to lead these changes in how we organise and do business. Do we need influential companies and organisations to lead the way and will we all eventually buy into it? Perhaps it could be a more organic process, as each one of us, in some small way, makes a deliberate vow to change the manner in which we do business; change the 'no' to a 'yes'; change the imbalance to harmony. Okay, I'm idealistic, but if everyone took a single step in the right direction, it would have to make a difference. It is not accidental that I have had access to some amazing individuals on my WMB journey. It is, however, surprising. I didn't deliberately launch a title for businesswomen in the anticipation that I would encounter such influential women along the way. I had thought that by promoting women I was leveling the media playing pitch, thus introducing role models into the arena. It was a simple, straightforward and honest aspiration. The bonus is realising that my goals have brought me in contact with change makers who have inspired me to think bigger – they have helped me to expand my thought horizon.

Women of Change

One such person is the first lady of football Karren Brady, vice-chairman of West Ham United, who spoke so passionately at our Annual Conference in September 2008. The 'LOL' moment for me was when she admitted to selling her husband, Paul Peschisolido, not once, but twice – not possible for most women unless their husband happens to be a footballer of course! Karren possesses the rare quality of confidence and conviction with a helping of good humour. Her credentials are so impressive that on first view you can't help but feel that you've underachieved. Brady got my vote when, as Lord Sugar's right-hand woman, she intervened in what could be best described as a verbal cat fight amongst the would-be female apprentices in one of the episodes of *The Apprentice*. It was a 'cringe' moment for all on-lookers, especially women, and fortunately Brady, professionally and with poise, put them immediately in check when she reminded them: 'You have to remember who you're representing in this process – young women out there who want to have an opportunity to do this. You should be an example to them.' Under Brady's management of Birmingham City FC, the majority of senior management at direct level were women. And within a short time at West Ham she appointed three women to senior roles. So she really does 'walk the talk'. In an interview last year, Brady admitted that she loves the title 'working women' because it suits her down to the ground: 'I work and I'm a mother and these are the two most important things in my life.' She is one charismatic woman who continues to balance the playing pitch in the gender fight.

Julie Meyer is founder of Ariadne Capital and Entrepreneur Country. Regarded as an entrepreneurial champion, Meyer was the keynote speaker at our Annual Conference 2010. Ariadne Capital has pioneered a new model for the financing of entrepreneurship – entrepreneurs backing entrepreneurs. Meyer founded Ariadne in 2000, with the backing of fifty-seven founding investors, amongst whom are the founders of some of the most successful Internet and technology companies in recent history. With a reputation for working with game changers in technology and media start-up work, it is not surprising that Meyer's credentials impress – I mentioned her numerous awards and achievements in Chapter 7. She is definitely a woman who stands out from the crowd. One of Meyer's more recent passions is setting up a 'Dads and Daughters' foundation to support and extend her thesis that women's identities are shaped – for good or bad – by the messages they receive from their fathers as children and young adults. I might make a good case study as, although I was only directly influenced by my father for seven short years, I have managed to fill the intervening void with lasting memories and lessons.

The last person who I believe is spreading the message of 'womenomics' and that change is needed is Avivah Wittenberg-Cox. Avivah also spoke at our Annual Conference and has written two books – *Why Women Mean Business* and *How Women Mean Business*. Avivah is passionate about the female talent pool and about the necessity for a bi-lingual approach to business. Her dedication in her most recent book says it all: 'To the men who care, the women who dare, and the companies (and countries) lighting the way.' Avivah is managing partner of 20-first, a consultancy firm that works with organisations to achieve gender balance. She is a consultant, coach, trainer and author, and she works with progressive companies interested in the female half of the talent pool and the market. In an interview with *WMB* (issue 23, pp. 40–43), Avivah spoke about how 'The old values – aggression, individualism, risk taking – have failed and it's time for something new and more effective.' Gender balancing brings the best mix of management styles to the fore and has a positive impact on the bottom line. She thinks that 'A greater emphasis is now being placed on the softer skills: motivation, teamwork, and inclusion. Naturally men will adapt and hone these skills over time but women tend to demonstrate them naturally.'

These three women have come across my path in my work with WMB. I've been fortunate to have met them, to have heard their stories and to have been inspired by their desire to make a difference. These women are incredible role models and mentors.

There are, of course, fantastic women in Ireland who are paving the way for women in business. Business leaders and change makers in the media spotlight include Anne Heraty, Cathriona Hallahan, Tina Roche, Caroline Casey – the list is endless. The media has its role to play, not only in highlighting the inequalities that exist in business, but in offering informed debate on the matter. In fact, many of our media influencers are women – Geraldine Kennedy, Miriam O'Callaghan and Marian Finucane, with a new crop coming up the ranks hot on their professional heels.

However, lest you feel I'm being too gender biased, men have a huge role to play in our change agenda. Many have joined in to right the inadequacies of our antiquated and unfair systems. These men can be found changing nappies at dawn, doing the school run, employing the best 'person' for the job, ensuring salary scales are transparent, delivering a clear message at the boardroom table, debating for change at government level. Yes, they are our partners and fathers, businessmen and leaders, visionaries and friends. I may have launched WMB to put a spotlight on our businesswomen and female entrepreneurs, which is a worthy objective. However, both men and women will lead the change necessary in the coming decades.

The Gender Shift – A 'to do' list

- *More female representation needed at a political level.* As the *Guardian* debates the 'Progressive Decline of Women in Politics', and the *Washington Post* poses the question 'Are

Women in Politics Taking Two Steps Forward, One Step Back?'
I remain disillusioned in the wake of our last general election
at the meagre female representation that has resulted. Women
represent almost 50 per cent of the population, and can therefore exercise significant voting power. However, out of 166
seats, 141 of these went to men and 25 to women, representing
just 15 per cent of the overall figure, one of the lowest percent-
ages of female representation in the world. This is a marginal
increase on our previous election's results, which saw female
political representation stand at 13 per cent.

- *More female representation required at board level.* We've all read
the headlines and it paints a pretty pathetic picture. Almost half
of the FTSE 250 companies do not have a single woman in the
boardroom. The UK Government has put this issue firmly in
the spotlight in that it proposes that FTSE 100 companies
should aim for a 25 per cent female representation on their
boards by 2015 – a voluntary ask for the moment. According to
the *2010 Catalyst Census: Fortune 500 Women Board Directors*
report, women held just 15.7 per cent of board seats – half of a
percentage point gain on 2009 figures. At this rate, women will
continue to polish the table rather than shine at its head.

- *Close the gender pay gap.* It is estimated that women earn
anything between 10 and 17 per cent less than their male
counterparts. According to the UK *Annual Survey of Hours and
Earnings*, the full-time gender pay gap, as measured by the
median hourly pay excluding overtime, narrowed by two
percentage points between 2009 and 2010. For full-time
employees, the pay gap is 10.2 per cent, down from 12.2 per
cent in 2009. This is the biggest fall in the gender pay gap since
the measure was first produced in 1997. For part-time employees, the gap has widened in favour of women, extending to
minus 4 per cent, compared with minus 2.5 per cent in 2009
(UK Office for National Statistics). These results are encouraging, but still you have to wonder why there is a gap at all! The
women of Dagenham fought for equal pay back in the 1960s

and they found a politician – Barbara Castle – who shared their feelings for fairness, which culminated in the Equal Pay Act of 1970. Who is our Barbara Castle of the twenty-first century?

- *A balanced approach to child care.* Women are fortunate to experience motherhood in all its facets. Although we are stretched both physically and emotionally by the process, the gift of childbirth has no comparison. However, women need to be true to themselves as they juggle the roles of carer and career girl. Look at women in education – over 60 per cent of EU university graduates are female. What happens to this fantastic talent pool, as women certainly aren't represented at decision-making levels? Out of choice, many women decide to opt out of the race in exchange for a more balanced life. Others want to continue on their career paths but are knocked back continuously. Only when men can and want to take on a greater role in child rearing will the status quo change. I'm not advocating increased maternity leave for women. I am strongly in favour of leave being shared between both parents. No one gets left behind, no single career is compromised and a child benefits from both parents in the process.

- *More visible female role models.* The adage 'Seeing is believing' comes to mind. Unless we see a big increase in female role models across the various disciplines, particularly in the area of technology and science, very little will change. Our daughters will only aspire to less 'traditional' paths in life if they are encouraged by example. With huge respect to the men that I do admire, it has been a 'man's world' for far too long – it is time for change.

Following a 'to do' list like this would help us get back on our feet and accelerate economic recovery.

In all the time that I have been in business, I have received very little financial support in the process. In the good days, it was because I didn't really need it. When I initially went to the bank for a loan, I was politely refused, even though I had a good financial track record for many years and vast experience. I could, however, get an overdraft facility, provided it was personally guaranteed. Isn't it amazing the way in which bankers were able to get such security out of the little people, while, at the same time, advancing millions with a 'wink and a nod' to our now defunct developers? Yes, life, my friend, isn't fair and you can moan about it or you can do something about it. I work, like many other self-employed businesspeople, on my wits. I am a slave to my cash flow projections as I fight to maintain a positive attitude and clear business vision. So, on pondering the thought of change and in tandem with the necessity to see a gender shift, I have committed to print what I would do if given the reins of power. An unlikely scenario, I know, but anything is possible! Some thoughts may seem radical, some pure fantasy, but, as Nelson Mandela once reflected, 'A good head and a good heart are always a formidable combination.'

A Time for Change – A Wish List

- *Education.* Our system sucks. At its worst, it saps any creative energy out of students in the name of textbook learning and doesn't encourage entrepreneurial spirit or individuality. Get rid of transition year – it's the greatest excuse to doss and is an unnecessary cost to the Exchequer and to those privileged enough to be in private education. Instead, replace this year with an optional internship year on completion of school. Allow companies (public and private sector) to embrace the availability of a spare pair of hands, while ensuring that the interns are gaining valuable experience. Companies would pay the unemployment social welfare rate applicable to the candidate. Most importantly, entrepreneurship should be included as a subject on the school curriculum and should be structured to include talks by successful entrepreneurs.

- *Social accountability.* We know there's a culture of fraud operating within our social welfare system but don't ask me to prove it! There should be zero tolerance for the fraudsters. A social and community aspect to 'social welfare' is essential and anyone who is long-term unemployed should be actively engaged at some level of society. Depression, lack of self-worth and illness are all symptoms of being unemployed. We should tackle these issues head-on and involve the working population in the solution.

- *Apartheid.* I use this term as it has all the negative connotations of an 'us' and 'them' mentality, for instance, the public versus the private sector; men versus women; rich versus poor. Two perspectives are better than one. It's about time that we worked together instead of blaming one another.

- *Funding.* There are only so many ways you can ask the question 'Where did all the cash go?' As start-ups are starved of that all-important seed capital, there is a real need to encourage those with private cash to become business angels.

- *Entrepreneurial tap.* We're a small country with huge expertise and even greater resilience. It's about time that successful businessmen and women were called on for their expert advice at government level. Advertise to entrepreneurs for submissions where no remuneration is payable. If they are successful enough, they'll want to make a difference and won't need the money.

- *Ireland, the island of saints and scholars.* Given the bad press over recent years, our island needs to be put into a new context as we're no longer saints and we've also fallen down the educational league tables. We need to reinvent ourselves. It may be through tourism; it may be through cloud technology. But let's be decisive about our possibilities and embrace the process.

When I launched WMB Publishing, I wrote a note to myself on what I envisaged for my new business. It is all of 125 words in length and I signed it, thus committing myself as with any contract. It sits in one of my many notebooks and reveals itself at the most opportune times – usually when I'm flying off in different directions with loads of ideas and no real focus.

My business idea is to create a multi-media platform for business-women and female entrepreneurs and for those wishing to connect with this target market. I want my brand to empower, motivate and promote women in a networking environment. The business will have several platforms (mag/web/conference/awards). My business will be called WMB Media Ltd (working title) and I will succeed because of my extensive publishing experience, media knowledge, first mover position, vision, contacts and unique offering.

The business will be successful because my target market is a growing segment that has been previously untapped. It is my desire that, within two years, the WMB brand will be at breakeven; in three years' time, it will turn the corner; and within five years, the business will be highly profitable.

Signed: Rosemary Delaney

I didn't realise when I wrote this that, two years down the line, Ireland and the world would be walking into one of the worst recessions of our time. However, I kept my cool and worked really hard so that, five years down the line, I'm on target to make a profit, albeit not the big profit that I had envisaged when I started out. I have worked through many frustrating experiences – lack of human resources, lack of finance, anxiety and uncertainty. I have grown as an individual but I've also lost the more carefree side to myself. This could be down to the business or it could just be down to life – becoming a wife, a mother, a caretaker, an employer, a forty-something. It's most likely to be a combination of all these things.

An entrepreneur's journey is not for the faint hearted. I'm travelling an unknown road full of possibilities that really excite me and also scare me. I have programmed my sat-nav to take me to success. I will have to take a couple of detours along the way, but one thing is certain – I'm not travelling this road alone.

Further Reading

Chua, Amy (2011), *Battle Hymn of the Tiger Mother*, London, UK: Bloomsbury.

Cranfield University School of Management (2010), *The Female FTSE Board Report 2010*, available at: http://www.som.cranfield.ac.uk.

Gray, John (2001), *Children Are from Heaven: Positive Parenting Skills for Raising Cooperative, Confident and Compassionate Children*, Whitby, UK: Quill Publishing.

Guardian, The (2011), 'Women in Politics: Progressive Decline', 2 May, available at: www.guardian.co.uk.

Hill, Napolean (2008), *Think and Grow Rich*, revised edition, London, UK: Vermilion.

Hill, Napoleon and Stone, W. Clement (1991), *Success through a Positive Mental Attitude: Discover the Secret of Making Your Dreams Come True*, London, UK: Thorsons.

Jardine, Cassandra (2010), 'Babies Are Better Late than Never', *Telegraph*, 27 May 2010, available at: http://www.telegraph.co.uk.

Leach, Penelope (2010), *Your Baby and Child*, London, UK: Dorling Kindersley.

Marcus, Ruth (2011), 'Are Women in Politics Taking Two Steps Forward, One Step Back?' *Washington Post*, 6 April, available at: www.washingtonpost.com.

Murphy, Joseph (2008), *The Power of Your Subconscious Mind: Unlock Your Master Key to Success*, Radford, US: Wilder Publications.

O'Doherty, Michael (2009), *Just Imagine ... A Life without Illness*, Dublin, Ireland: Blackwater Press.

Parsons, Rob (2009), *The Sixty Minute Mother*, London, UK: Hodder & Stoughton.

Pausch, Randy (2010), *The Last Lecture: Lessons in Living*, London, UK: Hodder Paperbacks.

Redfield, James (1994), *The Celestine Prophecy: An Adventure*, London, UK: Bantam.

Simmons School of Management (2009), *Risky Business: Busting the Myth of Women as Risk Averse*, Centre for Gender in Organisations, Briefing Note Number 28, April, available at: www.simmons.edu.

The Future Laboratory (2009), *The Rise of Lipstick Entrepreneurs*, report commissioned by Avon Cosmetics with a contribution from the Federation of Small Businesses.

Tolle, Eckhart (2001), *The Power of Now: A Guide to Spiritual Enlightenment*, London, UK: Hodder Paperbacks.

Wittenberg-Cox, Avivah (2010), *How Women Mean Business: A Step-by-Step Guide to Profiting from Gender Balanced Business*, Chichester, UK: John Wiley & Sons.

Wittenberg-Cox, Avivah and Maitland, Alison (2009), *Why Women Mean Business*, Chichester, UK: John Wiley & Sons.